Confederate Monuments

Revisiting Our History

Art and Its Destruction

DEDICATION

To the professor who made this all worthwhile,
thank you Kelley for introducing us to art history.
This semester will be a tough act to follow.

CONTENTS

ACKNOWLEDGMENTS

Thank you to Professor Kelley Helmstutler-Di Dio, who recognized a unique opportunity in the state of our country for art history students studying destruction of art. Without her guidance and leadership this project would not have been finished, and definitely would not have begun.
Thank you to the hardworking students in HCOL 185: Art and Its Destruction, who took this project on with a willingness and tenacity that went above and beyond initial expectations.

Special mentions for
Our general editors:
Zoë Kalbag, Erin Varnum, Cali Murray, and Meagan Cummins.
Our text editors:
Emily Connolly, Ally Merrill, and Kate Bamberger.
Our image editors:
Joscie Norris, Cali Murray, and Sarah Boller.
Our citation editors:
Zoë Kalbag and Kyle McLaughlin.
Our layout designers:
Erin Varnum, Cali Murray, and Meagan Cummins.

We are grateful to the University of Vermont's Honors College for providing the funds for this work to be published.

PREMISE

The Fall 2017 University of Vermont Honors College seminar, Art and Its Destruction, examined the complex issues involved in the looting, destruction and dismantling of art, diving deep into how and why art is a powerful tool of war and protest. In the months leading up to the start of the course, debate increased across the country regarding the monuments to the Confederacy found across the country. While some have argued the monuments were a reflection of southern heritage, others have argued that the monuments were entirely a reflection of white supremacists' desire to remind viewers of their dominance and continued discriminatory views in (especially, but not exclusively) Southern culture. Some have argued the monuments should be destroyed, others have argued they should be preserved either on site or in another setting, like a museum, battlefield, or cemetery. The debates came to a fore just a week before our course began, as clashes in Charlottesville in and around the area where a monument to Robert E. Lee stands reignited long-standing debates regarding the purposes and subtexts of these monuments to the losing side of the Civil War.

Kelley Helmstutler-Di Dio, Ph.D.

Professor of Art History

INTRODUCTION

"Who controls the past controls the future. Who controls the present controls the past."

George Orwell, 1984

One of the greatest conflicts in American history, the Civil War, was motivated by slavery and a desire to maintain the country's unity. This event brought to the surface one of the most divisive issues in the United States: racial equality. The conflict still permeates the country today, and its presence is reflected through its Confederate monuments.

Confederate statues are spread throughout the United States, especially in the Southern states, and they have provoked various responses from people around the nation. Some feel that these statues are a part of American history, acting as a commemoration of valiant soldiers, but others feel they are symbols of racial oppression. Many of these statues were created decades after the end of the Civil War, in the heart of the Jim Crow era. Forced to interact with the black community in a way they hadn't previously, white Southerners proclaimed their continued support of slavery with mass-produced, and often privately-funded, monuments honoring the soldiers and generals of the Confederacy. While many Southerners still see these monuments as representations of their heritage, minorities view them as representations of the hate-filled racial oppression of the early 1900s and of the challenges they still face in the modern United States.

For these reasons, art scholars and historians have debated whether these monuments and statues can be considered "art." Art can take on many different meanings for different people, but in general, art is a labor of love through which an artist can express his or her beliefs. While the Confederate monuments undoubtedly express the beliefs of their creators, their mass-production and original intentions make their status as art more ambiguous. Similar artistic contradictions have come up during other pivotal moments in history. The fall of the Soviet Union in the 1980s brought into question monuments dedicated to Communist leaders, like those of Joseph Stalin. Additionally, Saddam Hussein's removal from power in Iraq in 2003 instigated violent reactions to his statues. Some statues were torn from their bases and destroyed in the streets, while others were preserved and moved to museums. In all of these cases, including the current debate about the Confederate statues, individuals arguing for both sides have made their voices known. Whether they rioted in the streets, wrote scholarly articles, or talked about the issue with family members around the dinner table, opinions have not stayed quiet.

Regardless of whether these statues and monuments are viewed as art or not, there is still a charged debate about where they belong. Do the Confederate monuments deserve to stay in their current, public spaces in the center of cities and small towns? Or should they be moved to museums, where they can act as educational tools rather than reminders of oppression? It's up to each individual to decide where they stand on this issue.

Bridget Higdon and Skylar Bouffard

1 CHARLOTTESVILLE, VIRGINIA

History of Charlottesville

Charlottesville, Virginia has been the home of racial tensions since the arrival of its first settlers. At first a small agrarian town, Charlottesville became an integral component in the history of the Civil War, especially as technology and the Confederacy grew. Though Charlottesville didn't become a city until 1888, its growth began in the mid 1700s. The first official churches were established in the 1800s, and the railroad system was built in 1850, providing the opportunity for further expansion.[1] In 1854, the first mayoral election was held. During the Civil War, the University of Virginia campus functioned as a hospital at which many wounded soldiers were treated. The city suffered from many personal losses during the war, as other states did, but its infrastructure was barely damaged. At the turn of the century, the rail and trolley systems developed, increasing the size of the city that remained agriculturally based. Housing and suburban areas also grew during this time, due to high demand, and tourism increased primarily because of the purchase of Monticello by the Thomas Jefferson Memorial Foundation.[2]

---

[1] "History of Charlottesville and Albemarle County," *Charlottesville Virginia Official Travel Site*, https://www.visitcharlottesville.org/about/history/

[2] "Charlottesville: A Brief Urban History," *The Institute for Advanced Technology in the Humanities*, 28 July 2005, http://www2.iath.virginia.edu/schwartz/cville/cville.history.html

Perhaps one of the most significant events in the production of conflicting beliefs regarding race within Charlottesville's history was the founding of the University of Virginia by Thomas Jefferson, a known slaveholder. The university was founded "on [his] contradictory ideological loyalties - his protection of state rights, his hypocritical views on slavery, and his bold, liberal vision for his university and the country".[3] Despite his desire to maintain separation between the university and the city life of Charlottesville, the city expanded towards the university, establishing the school as one of the most important aspects of the city. The students who first attended the University of Virginia were the children of white plantation farmers who brought racist beliefs with them, especially evident through their fighting against a rule preventing them from bringing their slaves to school.[4] In Charlottesville, "slaves outnumbered whites [...] until the Civil War".[5] As attendance increased, demand for housing nearby also increased, inspiring the growth of suburban areas around the university. The KKK had a chapter on campus, and it donated to the university's endowment in 1921. After World War II, the university grew in size, and as a result it became Charlottesville's largest employer. Black students weren't admitted into public colleges, including the University of Virginia, until 1968, despite the fact that there were laws in place prohibiting the segregation of schools.[6]

It's no secret that Charlottesville has experienced a history of racism, conflicting ideas regarding race and politics, and violence.

---

[3] Lauren Jackson, "White Supremacists Didn't Just Arrive in Charlottesville. They've Always Been There," *Washington Post*, 14 Aug. 2017, https://www.washingtonpost.com/news/posteverything/wp/2017/08/14/white-supremacists-didnt-just-arrive-in-charlottesville-theyve-always-been-there/?utm_term=.2b336c1914c4

[4] Ibid

[5] Ibid

[6] Doug Stafford, "Racism Never Died in Virginia," *Time*, 18 Aug. 2017, http://time.com/4906341/charlottesville-va-home-racism-confederacy/.

These issues still exist today, visible in the usage of racial slurs, the presence of white supremacist rallies, and the existence of conflicts about the Confederate monuments in Charlottesville. A city built on racism and slavery is bound to continue its struggle with these issues because people often cling to these past beliefs. The Confederate statues were "erected at times when whites in the South were particularly eager to assert white supremacy," proving that these statues weren't intended to educate, but rather to demonstrate the power that these figures held in order to continue their so-called legacy.[7] These symbolic statues commemorate a history of racism and violence, a history that should neither be forgotten nor repeated. Many people hold that these statues remain important as historical symbols, though many believe they symbolize deeper racism and tolerance. This conflict of beliefs shows that these statues do have a controversial history, and the fate of these statues is justly in question, though it is continually debated whether they should actually be taken down. The statues may represent an important and integral part of history, but they also represent racism and violence that still continues today.

Monuments in Charlottesville

The most important and striking statue in Charlottesville is that of Robert E. Lee in Emancipation Park, previously known as Lee Park. It was built partially by Henry Merwin Shrady, who died in the process, and was finished by Leo Lentelli.[8] It took seven years to complete, and was finally erected in 1924.[9] When it was unveiled

---

[7] Paul Waldman, "The Lie of Maintaining Confederate Monuments in the Name of 'History,'" *The Washington Post*, 22 Aug. 2017, www.washingtonpost.com/blogs/plum-line/wp/2017/08/22/the-lie-of-maintaining-confederate-monuments-in-the-name-of-history/?utm_term=.19d749d9bc05.

[8] Jacey Fortin, "The Statue at the Center of Charlottesville's Storm," *The New York Times*, 13 Aug. 2017, https://www.nytimes.com/2017/08/13/us/charlottesville-rally-protest-statue.html

[9] Ibid; "History and Gardens of Emancipation Park," *City of Charlottesville*, http://www.charlottesville.org/departments-and-services/departments-h-z/parks-

during a Confederate reunion on May 21, 1924, it was covered by a Confederate flag, a strong image that depicts how the history of Lee and his statue are rooted in the racist and nationalist ideals of the Confederacy.[10] This statue signifies General Lee's role in the Civil War, and has become an icon for the Confederacy that continues to be influential today.

The next most significant Confederate monument in Charlottesville is the equestrian statue of Thomas Jonathan "Stonewall" Jackson, which resides in Justice Park, formerly known as Jackson Park. Paul Goodloe McIntire purchased the land specifically for this park and statue to be built, and according to the deed, the land "will never be used other than for a park and [...] no other monument except Jackson's would ever occupy it".[11] McIntire commissioned sculptor Charles Keck to build the statue. During and after its erection, controversies about which direction it should face arose, but McIntire had the final say, and decided to keep it facing south, possibly as a way of paying homage to the Confederacy.[12] The statue was unveiled on October 19, 1921, during a Confederate reunion by Anna Jackson Preston, the great-great-granddaughter of Stonewall Jackson. Again, this statue of Stonewall Jackson symbolizes the roles he held in both the war and the Confederacy, a significance that continues today.

The existence of these Confederate statues, among others in Charlottesville, Virginia and the rest of the country, represents how

---

recreation-/parks-trails/city-parks/lee-park/history-and-gardens-of-lee-park.

[10] "History and Gardens of Emancipation Park," *City of Charlottesville*, http://www.charlottesville.org/departments-and-services/departments-h-z/parks-recreation-/parks-trails/city-parks/lee-park/history-and-gardens-of-lee-park.

[11] "Justice Park," *Cvillepedia*, 19 July 2017, http://www.cvillepedia.org/mediawiki/index.php/Justice_Park.

[12] Ibid; "History and Gardens of Justice Park," *City of Charlottesville*, http://www.charlottesville.org/departments-and-services/departments-h-z/parks-recreation-/parks-trails/city-parks/jackson-park/history-and-gardens-of-jackson-park

the remembrance of history can be continued through the construction of monuments, providing insight into why some racist ideals and issues remain plaguing Charlottesville today. The violence that occurred as a result of the continuous clash of race-based beliefs has resulted in the deaths and injuries of many people over the years. This may be proof that something needs to be done about these statues that maintain significance in the history of the United States.

Modern Examples

Like many of the other cities in which Confederate statues reside, Charlottesville has been engrossed in debates regarding the appropriate fate of their monuments. The two most prominent statues, those of Robert E. Lee in Emancipation Park and Thomas Jonathan "Stonewall" Jackson in Justice Park, represent the main focuses of these debates. In September 2017, the city of Charlottesville decided to tear down the statue of "Stonewall" Jackson "as soon as possible".[13] They recommended that "it be sold or transferred somewhere that will put it on display for educational, historical or artistic purposes".[14] The statue of Robert E. Lee is also to be taken down, according to a three to two vote by the City Council. The decision to remove the statues also involved "[selling] each statue to the highest bidder and [requiring] the buyer to arrange and pay for the removal".[15] While the debates and legal issues around taking them down continue, the statues were both covered in black tarps as a way of showing that the city was mourning the death

---

[13] Max Jaeger, "Charlottesville Council Votes to Remove 'Stonewall' Jackson Statue," *New York Post*, 6 Sept. 2017, https://nypost.com/2017/09/06/charlottesville-council-votes-to-remove-stonewall-jackson-statue/.

[14] Ibid

[15] Paul Duggan, "Battle over Robert E. Lee Statue in Hands of Charlottesville Judge," *The Washington Post*, 1 Sept. 2017, www.washingtonpost.com/local/public-safety/battle-over-robert-e-lee-statue-enters-charlottesville-courtroom-friday/2017/08/31/e2d94e1c-8ebb-11e7-84c0-02cc069f2c37_story.html?utm_term=.6cd93b058cbf.

of Heather Heyer, who was killed by a car driving through a crowd of people counter-protesting a white nationalist rally.[16] Given available resources, it seems that the statues have not yet been taken down, but actions have been taken to begin the process of their removal. The people's request to rid Charlottesville of these statues with a controversial history has been heard.

Emma Roach

[16] AnneClaire Stapleton and Eric Levenson, "Charlottesville Covers Confederate Monuments with Black Tarp," *Cable News Network*, 24 Aug. 2017, www.cnn.com/2017/08/23/us/charlottesville-monument-cover-fabric-trnd/index.html.

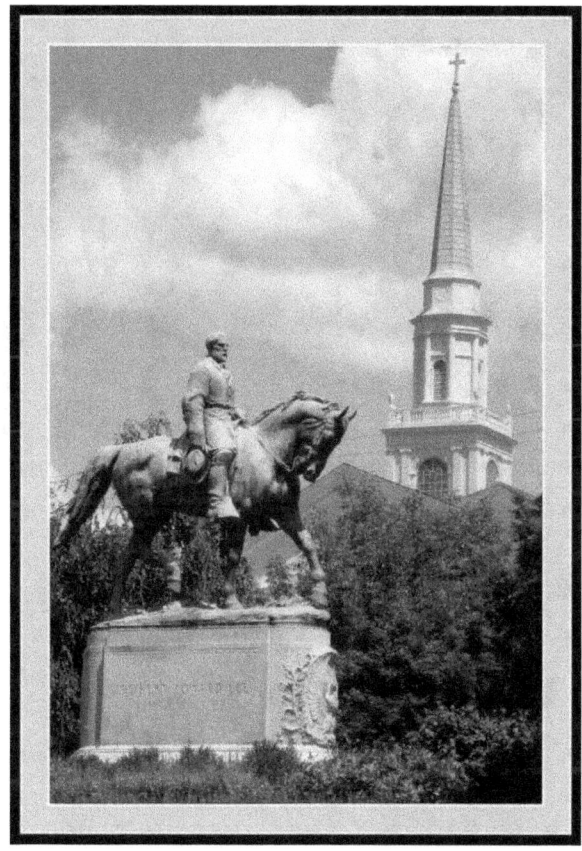

Robert E. Lee Statue in Emancipation park[17]

[17] Henry Shrady and Leo Lentelli. *Robert E. Lee.* 1924. Bronze statue. Lee Park, Charlottesville, Virginia. Available from: Flickr Commons, Bill McCheseny, https://www.flickr.com/photos/bsabarnowl/2744254199/in/photolist-5bv2az-dA5pTk-dAdr25-dAcn86-dAdqmG-dAdrL9-dA7Yat-WvMgaC-dA7XZ6-WvMgvY-hAX2ur-hAXaWs-6XytZK-hAWXvW-hAWRra-hB4MCc-hB3kkX-e6L3Rn-hB3R6C-Ws9ffy-hB3Ayb-hB2V52-5nqzoa-hB4L1e-hB4tST-Xu3m9r-hAY8Bn-WupAtB-hAYCwu-hB3TDd-5bPfGe-hB3rBA-X7TGnq-BaVxmj-XHW15a-hB3fTS-hAX9PM-5bTwoh-5bPaw8-hAZNLn-XvJPpn-5bPfwi-XvJDnP-Wupuzn-XDP65E-h

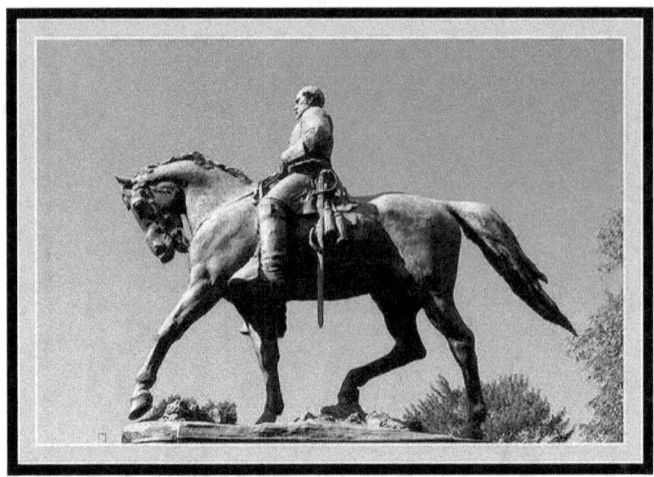

Robert E. Lee Statue in Emancipation Park[18]

---

[18] Henry Shrady and Leo Lentelli. *Robert E. Lee.* 1924. Bronze statue. Available from: Flickr Commons, Bill McCheseny,
https://www.flickr.com/photos/bsabarnowl/2745012684/in/photolist-5bv2az-5byUSS-5byXuf-5buBwH-5buBic-5bv224-5byWVf-5buFkn-5buEmB-5buB4k-5bySpQ-5bySPh-5buEvz-5buCAB-5byVrQ-5byUuo-e8Htx7-5buCpt-5buAyx-5byXC7-5bBZom-5byUCU-5buF6z-XFNyfG-5byXQQ-5buEAX-5buARx-5buzx4-5byT1w-5buDaF-9BeYEu-XUYUcB-XE2dTs-XKe5TD-5buBG8-5bySDs-5buBpK-5byVCQ-5buE6e-5byWqj-5buDpr-5buzgH-5buDxB

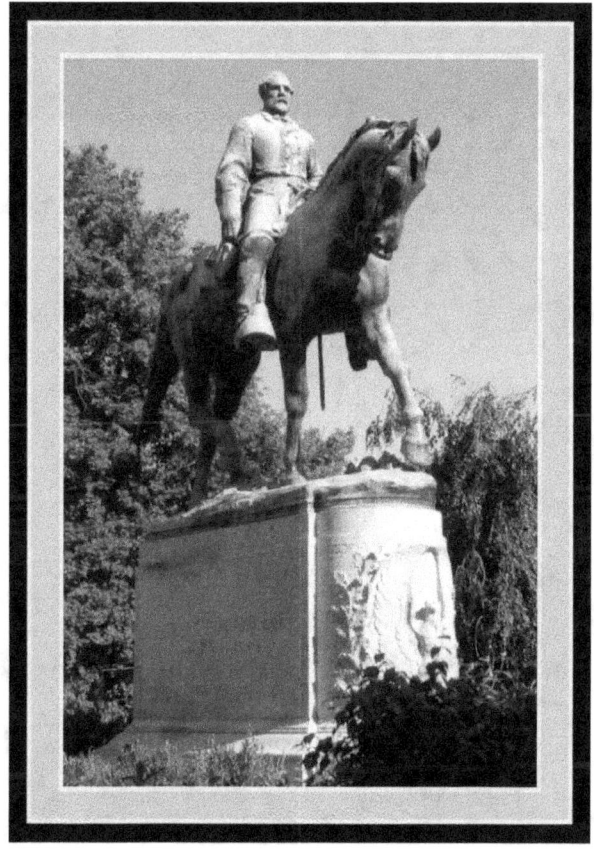

Robert E. Lee Statue in Emancipation Park[19]

[19] Henry Shrady and Leo Lentelli. *Robert E. Lee.* 1924. Bronze statue. Available from: Flickr Commons, Bill McCheseny,
https://www.flickr.com/photos/bsabarnowl/2745015406/in/photolist-5bv2az-5byUSS-
5byXuf-5buBwH-5buBic-5bv224-5byWVf-5buFkn-5buEmB-5buB4k-5bySpQ-5bySPh-
5buEvz-5buCAB-5byVrQ-5byUuo-e8Htx7-5buCpt-5buAyx-5byXC7-5bBZom-
5byUCU-5buF6z-XFNyfG-5byXQQ-5buEAX-5buARx-5buzx4-5byT1w-5buDaF-
9BeYEu-XUYUcB-XE2dTs-XKe5TD-5buBG8-5bySDs-5buBpK-5byVCQ-5buE6e-
5byWqj-5buDpr-5buzgH-5buDxB

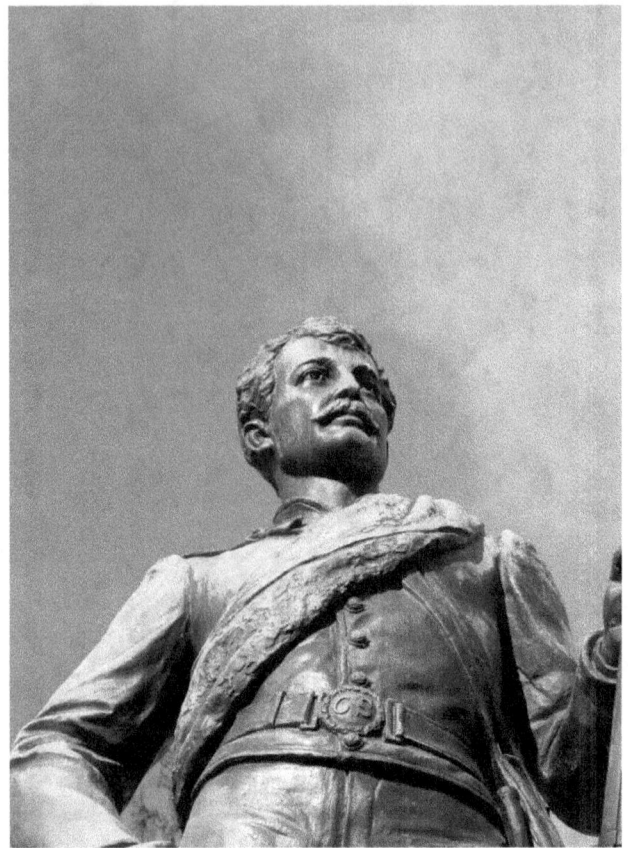

Civil War Memorial in the UVA Cemetery[20]

[20] *Civil War Memorial.* 1873. Bronze statue. UVA Cemetery, Charlottesville, Virginia. Available from: Flickr Commons, Bill McCheseny, https://www.flickr.com/photos/bsabarnowl/10898524463/in/photolist-5bv2az-hAX2ur-hAXaWs-hAWXvW-hAWRra-hB4MCc-hB3kkX-hB3R6C-5nqzoa-hB3Ayb-hB2V52-WvMgaC-hB4L1e-hB4tST-hAY8Bn-hAYCwu-hB3TDd-WvMgvY-hB3rBA-hB3fTS-hAX9PM-hAZNLn-hAXv6Y-hB3NfN-zmzdmG-zmze5A

2 RICHMOND, VIRGINIA

History of Richmond

When the statues on Monument Avenue were erected, Richmond was not in the immediate post-Civil War era. In the 1900s, Richmond was urbanizing. This caused closer encounters between people of different races as more people moved off of plantations and into congested cities. Inevitably, given the state's not too distant past, the development of new laws expressed racial discrimination. In 1902, Virginia's state constitution was amended to include poll taxes and literacy tests for voting rights, which significantly reduced the number of African American citizens that could vote. Segregation acts were passed to maintain or create separate residential areas, movie theaters, dance halls, and streetcars. In 1904, fifty years before Rosa Parks refused to give up her seat, there was a boycott of the Richmond streetcars. In the 1920s, the nationwide rise of both the KKK and the eugenics movement sparked the instatement of the Virginia Racial Integrity Act, which prohibited interracial marriages. Public officials feared speaking out against these laws and being labeled "negro lovers" because of the possibility of this reputation jeopardizing their positions.[21]

When the monument to General Lee was established in 1890, there were several African American city council members in

---

[21] "Overview of Race Relations in Virginia," *Jim Crow Lived Here*, jimcrowlivedhere.org/overview.

Richmond. These members refused to support funding for this statue. One city councilor, John Mitchell, wrote about how this monument was meant to memorialize the "Lost Cause", which was the romanticization of the Confederate cause as a heroic fight against great odds. Mitchell also argued that the monument represented what Richmond stood for during the Civil War, namely the preservation of the Southern way of life, rather than General Lee himself. He was particularly upset by the prominent placement, stating that it would provide a "legacy of treason and blood" to the future generations of Richmond.[22]

Maddie Bowe

Monuments in Richmond

Monument Avenue, an integral feature of Richmond, Virginia, was granted the honor of becoming a National Historic Landmark in 1997.[23] The avenue extends for five miles from Lombardy Street to Roseneath Road, a now coveted residential district lined with impressive townhouses, mansions, and churches.[24] However, the focal point of Monument Avenue is not the real estate, but the monuments. Five towering monuments honoring Confederate soldiers and contributors are situated along prominent intersections of the boulevard. Architect and author of *Richmond's Monument Avenue*, Robert Winthrop, said "[t]he street grew piece by piece. It turned into something different than what had been expected".[25]

---

[22] Tina Griego, "Past and Present: The Many-Sided History of the Monument Avenue Debate," *Richmond Magazine*, 25 June 2015, richmondmagazine.com/news/news/monument-ave-history/.

[23] "Monument Avenue Historic District: Landscape Information," *The Cultural Landscape Foundation*, tclf.org/landscapes/monument-ave-historic-district.

[24] Ibid

[25] Katherine Calos, "From the RTD Archives: History of Richmond's Monument Avenue," *Richmond Times-Dispatch*, 17 Aug. 2017, www.richmond.com/discover-richmond/from-the-rtd-archives-history-of-richmond-s-monument-avenue/article_14a657d0-937e-501d-ad83-40fe79df6df2.html.

In 1890, at the intersection of Allen and Monument Avenues, the intended centerpiece of the boulevard was revealed to the public. Jean Antoine Mercie's equestrian statue of Confederate General Robert Edward Lee became the first monument of Monument Avenue.[26] The Lee statue, unveiled 20 years after his death, continues to serve as the focal point of the avenue, resting at twenty-one feet on top of a forty-foot pedestal.[27] The placement of Mercie's dedication to the Confederate General inspired the commission of four more Confederate statues in the years that followed.

Two additional statues were presented to the public in 1907. The first, a monument of Confederate General James Ewell Brown Stuart, and the second, a monument commemorating Confederate President Jefferson Davis. Frederick Moynihan's equestrian statue of General J.E.B. Stuart was revealed at the intersection of Lombardy Street and Monument Avenue during a Confederate reunion in May of 1907.[28] Just days later in June, a monument of President Jefferson Davis, designed by William C. Noland and sculpted by Edward Valentine, was unveiled at the intersection of Davis and Monument Avenues. The Davis monument is regarded as particularly significant due to its placement at the former location of Star Fort, a Confederate station used throughout the Civil War.[29]

In 1919, Frederick William Sievers' statue of Confederate General Thomas Jonathan Jackson, more commonly known as Stonewall Jackson, was presented at the intersection of Boulevard

---

[26] Ibid

[27] "Monument Avenue Historic District," *National Parks Service*, www.nps.gov/nr/travel/richmond/monumentavehd.html.

[28] Katherine Calos, "From the RTD Archives: History of Richmond's Monument Avenue," *Richmond Times-Dispatch*, 17 Aug. 2017, www.richmond.com/discover-richmond/from-the-rtd-archives-history-of-richmond-s-monument-avenue/article_14a657d0-937e-501d-ad83-40fe79df6df2.html.

[29] "Monument Avenue Historic District: Landscape Information," *The Cultural Landscape Foundation*, tclf.org/landscapes/monument-ave-historic-district.

and Monument Avenues.[30] A decade later in 1929, Confederate scientist Matthew Fontaine Maury, rather than an additional Confederate soldier, was honored with a statue at the intersection of Belmont Street and Monument Avenue. This monument was Frederick William Sievers' second to be featured on the avenue.[31] After the dedication to Matthew Fontaine Maury, Monument Avenue remained untouched until 1996 when the succeeding statue was revealed. Unrelated to the Confederacy, the final monument honored Arthur Ashe, an African American civil rights leader and athlete.[32]

From honoring Confederate soldiers and slave owners to honoring an African American civil rights leader, Monument Avenue has gained the contextual history of an alternative perspective. The clash between and through racial lines has sparked controversy in Richmond. Richmond Mayor Levar Stoney candidly stated that the Confederate monuments "should be part of our dark past and not of our bright future".[33] Mayor Stoney proceeded to form the Monument Avenue Commission, a committee with the purpose of examining the potential to remove or relocate the statues. Robert Winthrop contributed to the debate by saying, "[t]here are different interpretations that go on over time. To put Ashe there continues the story".[34] Monument Avenue primarily serves as a

---

[30] Katherine Calos, "From the RTD Archives: History of Richmond's Monument Avenue," *Richmond Times-Dispatch*, 17 Aug. 2017, www.richmond.com/discover-richmond/from-the-rtd-archives-history-of-richmond-s-monument-avenue/article_14a657d0-937e-501d-ad83-40fe79df6df2.html.

[31] Ibid

[32] "Monument Avenue Historic District: Landscape Information," *The Cultural Landscape Foundation*, tclf.org/landscapes/monument-ave-historic-district.

[33] Daniella Silva,"Richmond Could Be Next Confederate Monument Battleground." *NBC News*, 20 Aug. 2017, www.nbcnews.com/news/us-news/richmond-could-be-next-confederate-monument-battleground-n793741.

[34] Katherine Calos, "From the RTD Archives: History of Richmond's Monument Avenue," *Richmond Times-Dispatch*, 17 Aug. 2017, www.richmond.com/discover-richmond/from-the-rtd-archives-history-of-richmond-s-

dedication to a misconstrued past; only now, a century after the construction of the Lee monument, is the conversation beginning to move forward.

Erin Varnum

monument-avenue/article_14a657d0-937e-501d-ad83-40fe79df6df2.html.

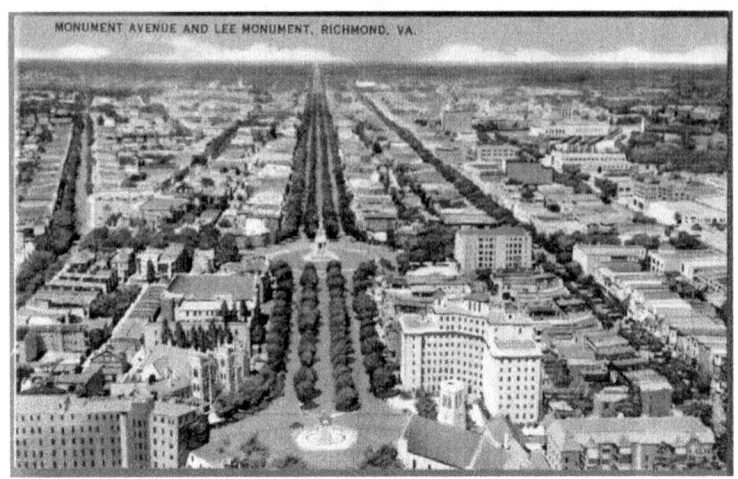

A View of Monument Ave[35]

---

[35] *Monument Avenue and Lee Monument.* Postcard. Richmond, Virginia. Available from: Flickr Commons, https://www.flickr.com/photos/vcucommons/16810945346/in/photolist-rBwunh-idhdrZ-rDR7oN-ouaiqJ-demVwT-ccFNoA-owP3Uk-i8y639-i7aXDk-kAWHKc-rDLsCS-bEcdzL-rkxGpD-i8mZNb-i8ju72-i7z6Xt-i8u5qe-UuzSrV-i8U1tY-i7pYqv-i8teeY-qGTuFs-hTSmn4-i8uCms-i6MBLY-RHNeKE-hVaJVa-hUx8YB-TV1RKj-YDXCVf-hTU9Fp-4y9nVD-od9CBS-owcVpP-ov3AsD-rngjm3-hQaDcg-oupkLD-i8cXJw-i8os7d-i21ht4-i8gBQx-i8dKEu-idGM81-hLXxE6-i8D8rW-r6ET8d-ek2qM4-qGRSaU-ow48Rn/

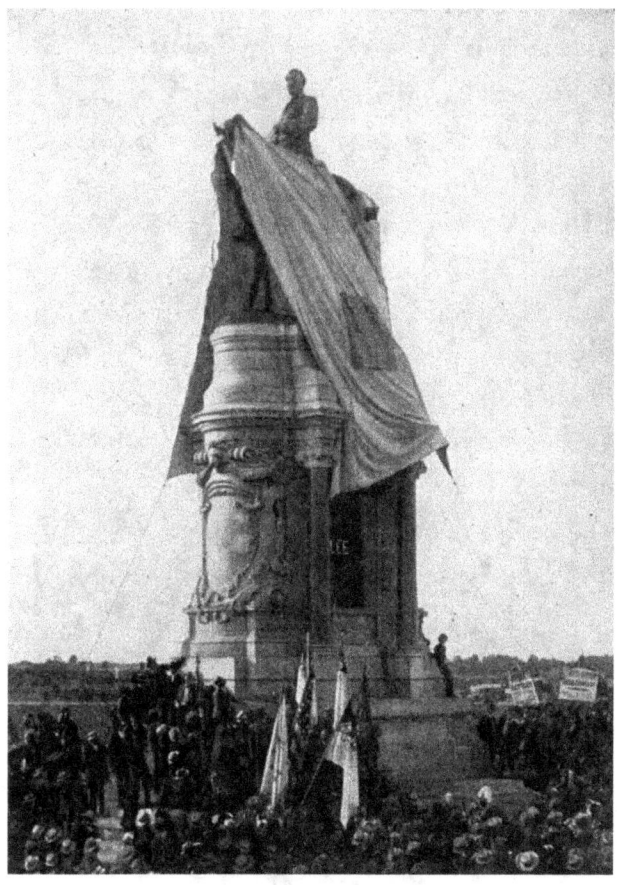

Unveiling of the Robert E. Lee on Monument Ave[36]

---

[36] *Unveiling of the Equestrian Statue of Robert E. Lee.* 29 May 1890. Photograph. Monument Avenue, Richmond, Virginia. Available from: Wikimedia Commons, E. Benjamin Andrews, https://commons.wikimedia.org/wiki/File:1890_Lee_statue_unveiling.jpg

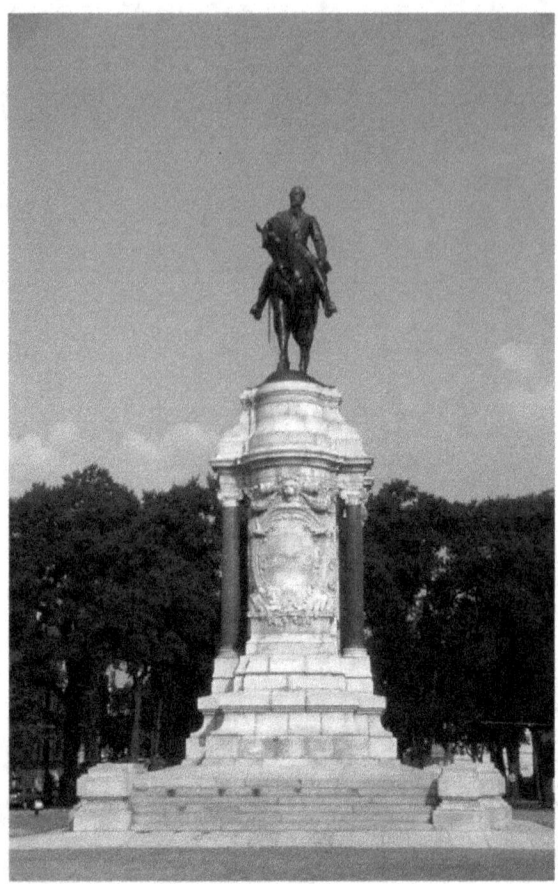

Robert E. Lee Statue on Monument Ave[37]

[37] Antonin Mercié. *Robert E. Lee.* 1890. Statue. Monument Avenue, Richmond, Virginia. Available from: Wikimedia Commons, Einar Einarsson Kvaran, GNU Free Documentation License https://commons.wikimedia.org/wiki/File:Mon-AveLee.jpg

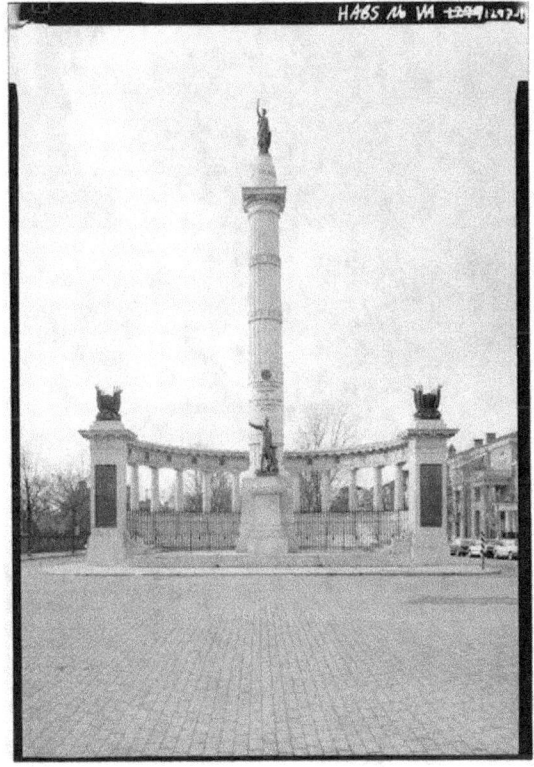

Jefferson Davis Statue on Monument Ave[38]

---

[38] Edward Valentine. *Davis Monument.* 1907. Statue. Monument Avenue, Richmond, Virginia. Available from: Wikimedia Commons, https://commons.wikimedia.org/wiki/File:EAST_SIDE_-_Davis_Monument,_Monument_Avenue_and_Davis_Avenue,_Richmond,_Independe nt_City,_VA_HABS_VA,44-RICH,146-1.tif

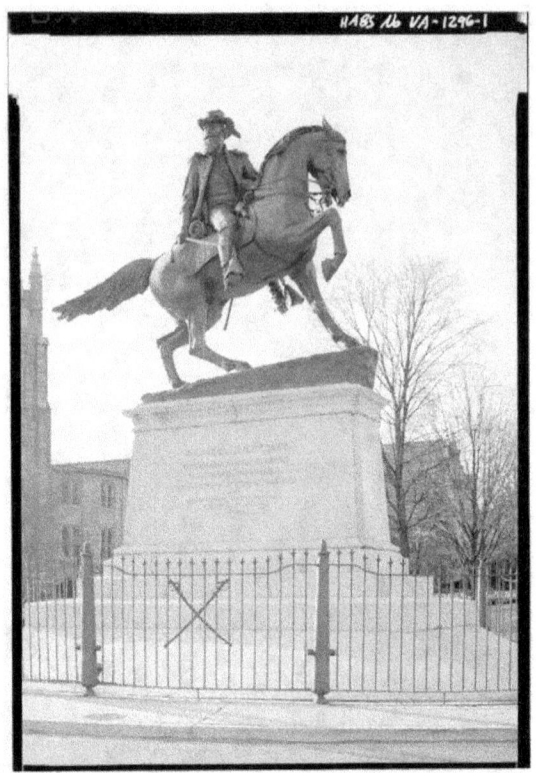

J.E.B. Stuart Statue on Monument Ave[39]

---

[39] Frederick Moynihan. *J.E.B. Stuart Monument.* 1904. Statue. Monument Avenue, Richmond, Virginia. Available from: Wikimedia Commons, https://commons.wikimedia.org/wiki/File:EAST_AND_NORTH_SIDES_-_Stuart_Monument,_Monument_Avenue_and_North_Lombardy_Street,_Richmond,_Independent_City,_VA_HABS_VA,44-RICH,149-1.tif

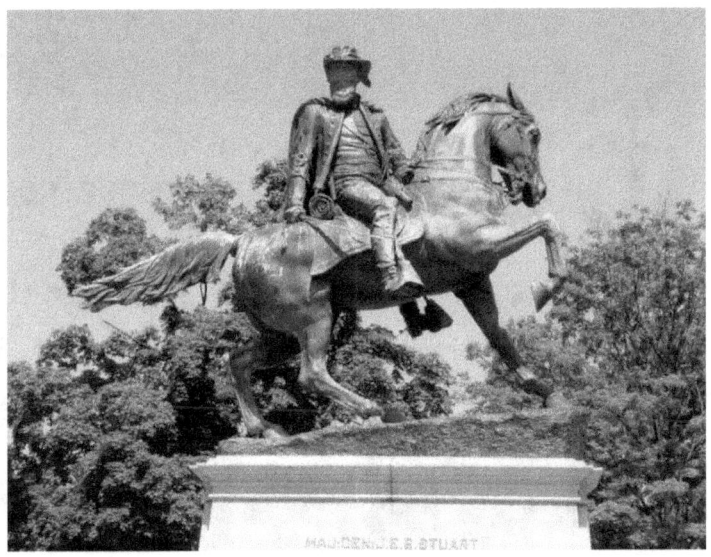

J.E.B. Stuart Statue on Monument Ave[40]

[40] Frederick Moynihan. *Statue of J.E.B. Stuart*. 1904. Statue. Monument Avenue, Richmond, Virginia. Available from: Wikimedia Commons, Hal Jespersen, https://commons.wikimedia.org/wiki/File:Monument_Ave_Jeb_Stuart.jpg

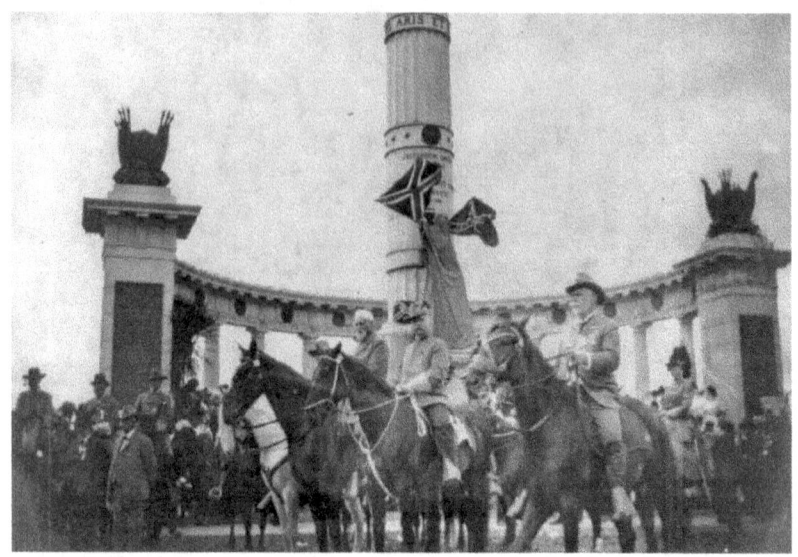

The Confederate Reunion Parade on Monument Ave, 1907[41]

[41] *George Washington Custis Lee in front of monument to Jefferson Davis.* 3 June 1907. Photograph. Richmond, Virginia. Available from: Wikimedia Commons, Edyth Carter Beveridge, https://commons.wikimedia.org/w/index.php?curid=10526230

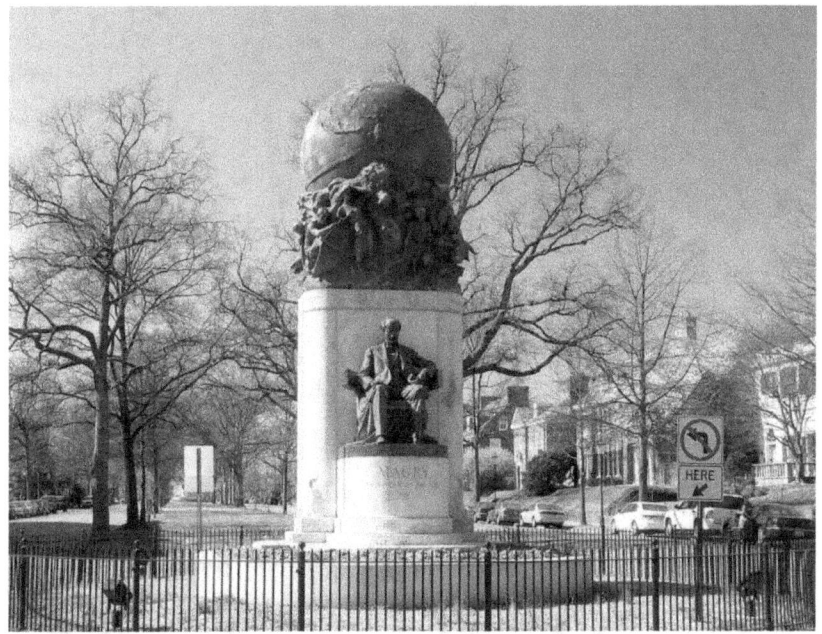

Monument to Mathew Fontaine Maury on Monument Ave[42]

[42] William F. Sievers. *Maury Statue.* 1929. Bronze and granite statue. Monument Avenue, Richmond, Virginia. Available from: Flickr Commons, Jim, https://www.flickr.com/photos/rvaphotodude/3127305176/in/photolist-5LmfSL-EBQShi-dG4Jg-5LmfHq

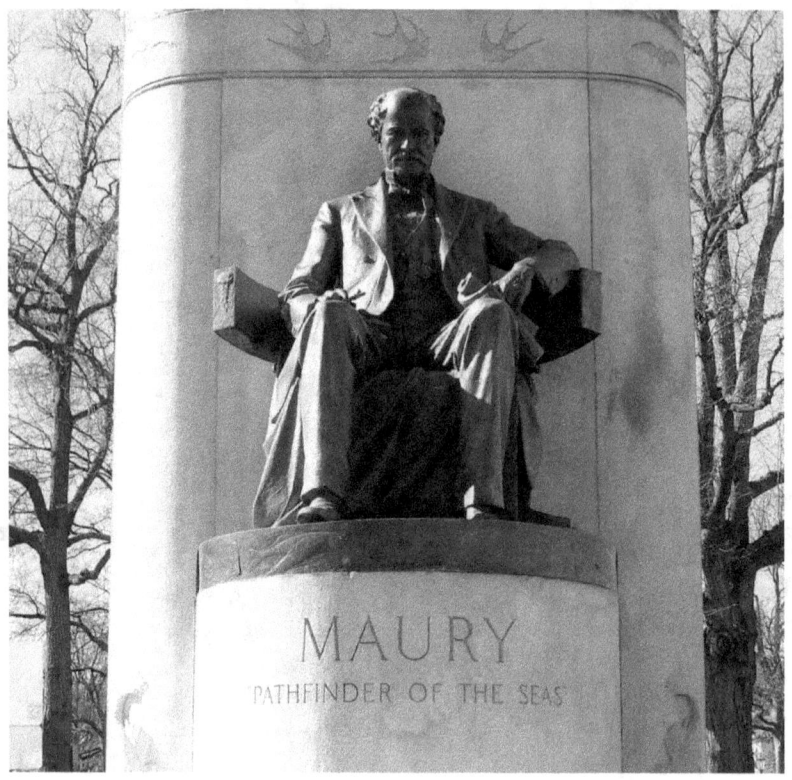

A Closer View of the Monument to Mathew Fontaine Maury[43]

[43] William F. Sievers. *Matthew Maury - Pathfinder of the Seas*. 1929. Bronze statue. Monument Avenue, Richmond, Virginia. Available from: Flickr Commons, Jim, https://www.flickr.com/photos/rvaphotodude/3127304634/in/photolist-5LmfSL-EBQShi-dG4Jg-5LmfHq

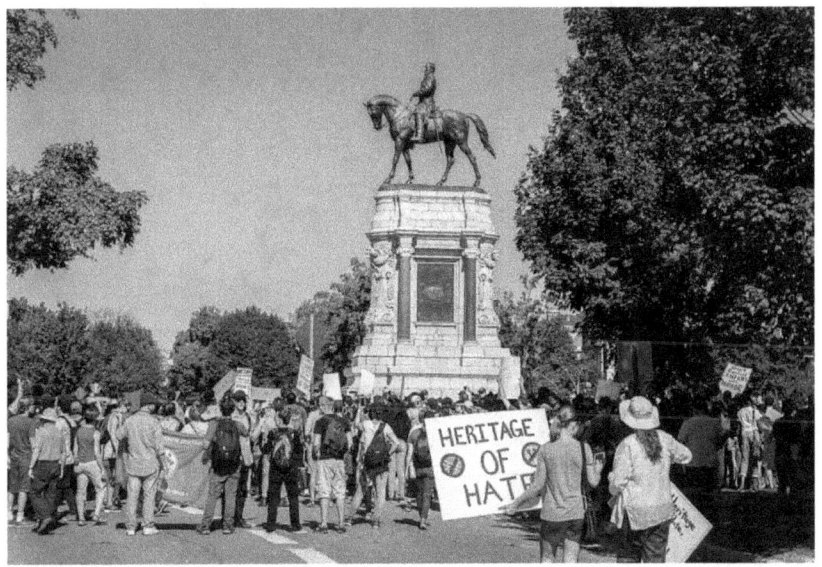

Counter Protesters at the Robert E. Lee Statue on Monument Ave[44]

---

[44] *Hundreds of marchers rally at the Robert E. Lee statue.* 16 Sept. 2017. Photograph. Monument Avenue, Richmond, Virginia. Available from: Wikimedia Commons, Mobilus In Mobili, Creative Commons Attribution-Share Alike 2.0 Generic license, https://commons.wikimedia.org/wiki/File:RVA_Counter-Protests_Against_New-CSA_(37109128732).jpg

3 BALTIMORE, MARYLAND

During the Civil War, Baltimore was under Union control and served as a transportation hub and supply depot for the Union army.[45] Because of its geographic location, Maryland depended greatly on both the South and the North for its local economy. Maryland remained as part of the Union throughout the war and ended up being very beneficial to the North. However, Maryland, as a border state, was not included in the emancipation proclamation, meaning that slaves within its borders were not, in fact, free. Public opinion during the months leading up to the war was heterogeneous. There was still a very large presence of Southern support in the city of Baltimore and as a result, it became known as a "mobtown".[46] President-elect Lincoln even had to alter his tour across America because of suspicion of a potential assassination plot that was planned to take place within the city.

Since Baltimore experienced such active involvement in the Civil War, the city, as a result, is saturated with Confederate monuments. After the deadly violence that took place in Charlottesville, four major Confederate statues were removed from the city of Baltimore. These removals took place overnight and gained a massive amount of media attention the following morning.

---

[45] "Baltimore in the Civil War," *Visit Baltimore*, baltimore.org/article/baltimore-civil-war.

[46] Ibid

The first statue was a bust of the allegorical figure Glory holding up a dying Confederate soldier that was once located on Mount Royal Avenue. Engraved in the statue was the quote "Gloria Victis" meaning "glory to the vanquished."

The second removed statue was a memorial to the women who aided the Confederacy during wartime, once located on West University Parkway. The statue showed two women caring for a dying soldier with the inscriptions "The Brave at Home" and "In difficulty and danger, regardless of self, they fed the hungry, clothe the needy, nursed the wounded, and comforted the dying."

The third statue depicted Robert E. Lee and Thomas J. "Stonewall" Jackson riding horses, and it could previously be found in Wyman Park Dell. The incorporation of equine imagery within the statue showed the power that these two men possessed during the Civil War. Below the statue there was an inscription that read, "They were great generals and Christian soldiers and waged war like gentlemen."

Lastly, the Roger B. Taney statue at Mount Vernon Place was taken down.[47] Taney was a Supreme Court Chief Justice and the author of the Dred Scott decision which ruled that black people were not to be considered citizens and that Congress could not regulate slavery. Even though Taney was not directly involved in the Civil War, it is clear that his stance on racial issues motivated his statue's removal.

Sean Quigley

---

[47] Jean Marbella and Colin Campbell, "Baltimore's Confederate Statues under Tarps as Trump, Stonewall Jackson Descendants Weigh In," *The Baltimore Sun*, 18 Aug. 2017, www.baltimoresun.com/news/maryland/baltimore-city/bs-md-ci-monuments-found-20170817-story.html.

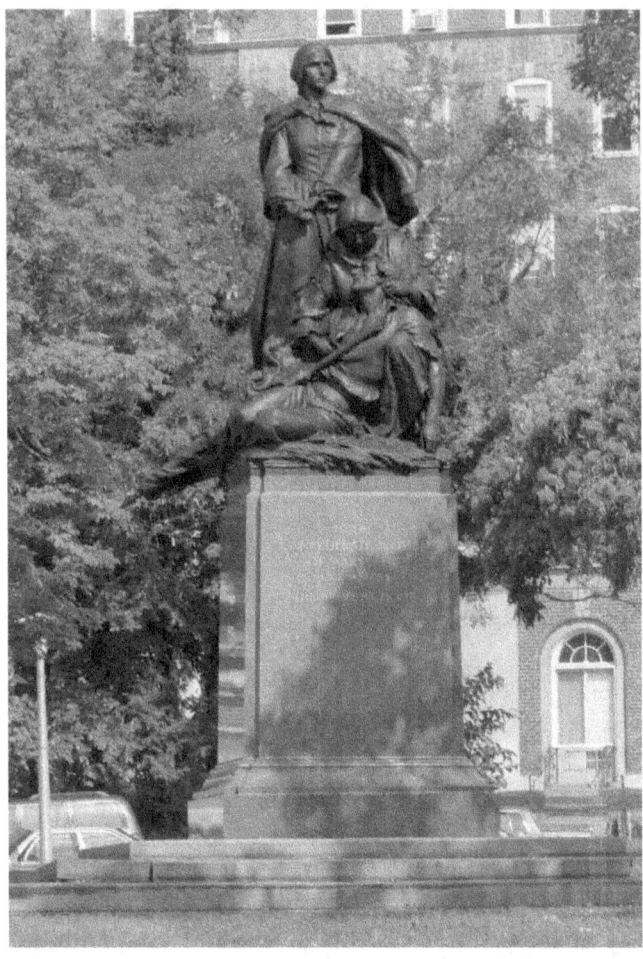

Confederate Women's Monument in Baltimore[48]

[48] Joseph Maxwell Miller. *Confederate Women's Monument.* 1917. Bronze statue. Baltimore, Maryland. Available from: Wikimedia Commons, https://upload.wikimedia.org/wikipedia/commons/0/08/CSAWomen2008.jpg

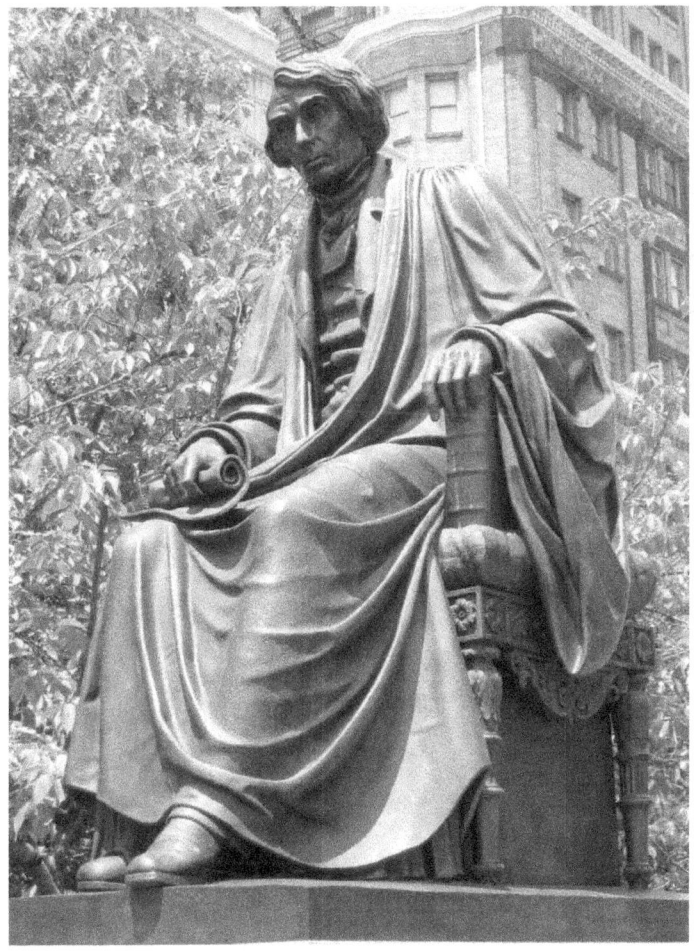

Rodger B. Taney Statue at Mount Vernon Place[49]

[49] William Henry Rinehart. *Robert B. Taney statue*. 1871. Statue. Mount Vernon Place, Baltimore, Maryland. Available from: Wikimedia Commons, https://commons.wikimedia.org/wiki/File:Roger_B._Taney_statue,_Mount_Vernon_Place,_Baltimore,_MD.jpg

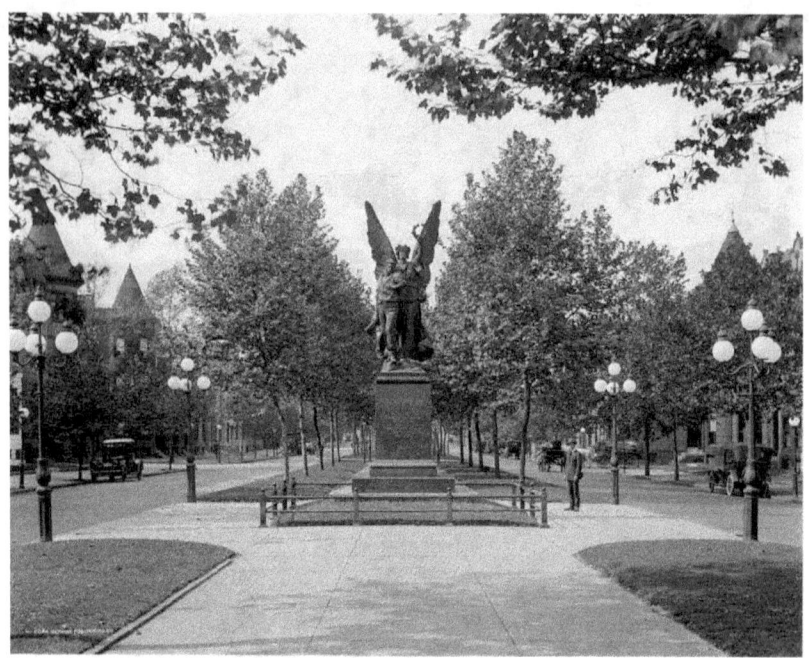

Confederate Soldiers and Sailors Monument[50]

[50] F. Wellington Ruckstuhl. *Confederate Soldiers and Sailors Monument.* 1902. Statue. Baltimore, Maryland. Available from: Wikimedia Commons, https://commons.wikimedia.org/wiki/File:Confederate_Soldiers_and_Sailors_Monume nt_Baltimore_1910.jpg

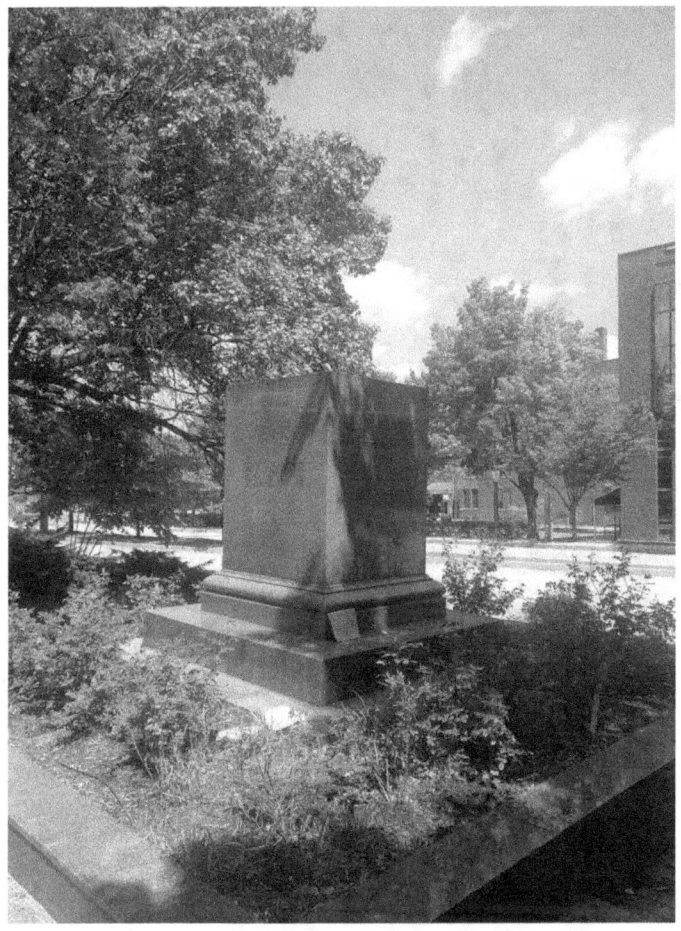

Empty Confederate Soldier and Sailors Statue Following its
Removal[51]

---

[51] *Pedestal after the removal of the Confederate Soldiers and Sailors Monument.*
19 Aug. 2017. Photograph. Baltimore, Maryland. Available from: Wikimedia
Commons, Vera de Kok,
https://commons.wikimedia.org/wiki/File:Pedistal_Confederate_Soldiers_and_Sailors_
Monument_(Baltimore,_Maryland)_Aug_2017_-_6.jpg

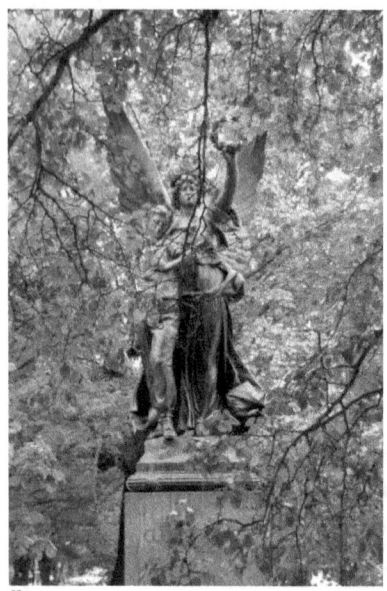
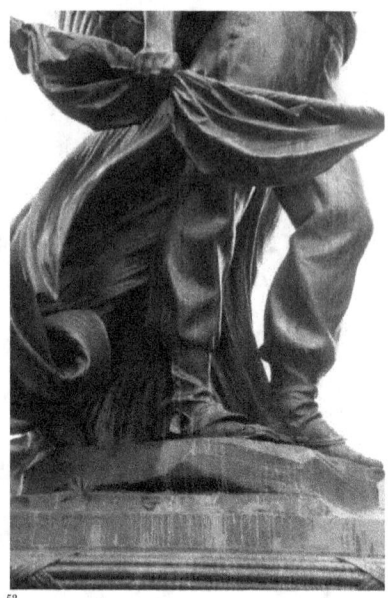

52   53

Graffiti on The Confederate Soldiers and Sailors Monument

[52] *Protest & Interventions at Confederate Monuments.* 7 Oct. 2015. Photograph. Baltimore, Maryland. Available from: Flickr Commons, Ryan Patterson, https://www.flickr.com/photos/baltimorepublicart/35764662443/in/photolist-Wupf86-XyULPp-WvhReY-XHWhy2-B9RFES-owseT5-icxKuW-oeYwNs-oeZ16y-oeZkfV-owcAcR-5qcTHG-owcGDP-XM6we2-ocMgTi-otFZ6m-odcCYM-XM8dJZ-qGRSaU-WvjJtG-oeZNVT-oeZ5NP-oux193-ouDpys-od3AG2-oeQEWX-ouv1N3-Xz5hUr-owhrbM-od3iNy-ocPMLv-owu6Ty-AAszgF-Af4Uyu-cHgv5h-owh7yY-owcMpR-ibX8t4-hWShfZ-ousjzA-owtJRB-icvRP4-aPeLMx-icACsn-id3bs5-oeZ7mY-owu6gz-oyeggR-i3EkXg-qGR56j

[53] *Protest & Interventions at Confederate Monuments.* 7 Oct. 2015. Photograph. Baltimore, Maryland. Available from: Flickr Commons, Ryan Patterson, https://www.flickr.com/photos/baltimorepublicart/36527512346/in/photolist-XHW15a-XvJPpn-XvJDnP-XDP65E-XDP3PC-XHWnCa-X7TyML-Ws9JuQ-WuprA6-Wupw9z-XHW34a-v4AnvE-XKe5TD-zmzdmG-X5WjYQ-X7TBro-XHWf2t-zmze5A-XDP4aC-WupBj4-Ws9edd-Wupf86-XHWgc4-XHWhy2-Xt3Ls3-WupzMM-Xt3Hhq-WupsXp-XHWjDp-WupxMV-XHVNZV-Wupz5e-XHVQ6c-XHVMjk-XDP4Do-XHW54T-Xt3K41-XHVLgi-X7TDT7-X7TJ6A-Wupbk6-XDP1Pq-XHWkLz-XDP3p9-XHW6V8-XDP36o-Wuphti-XvJN1F-Ws9cYu-X7TKLE

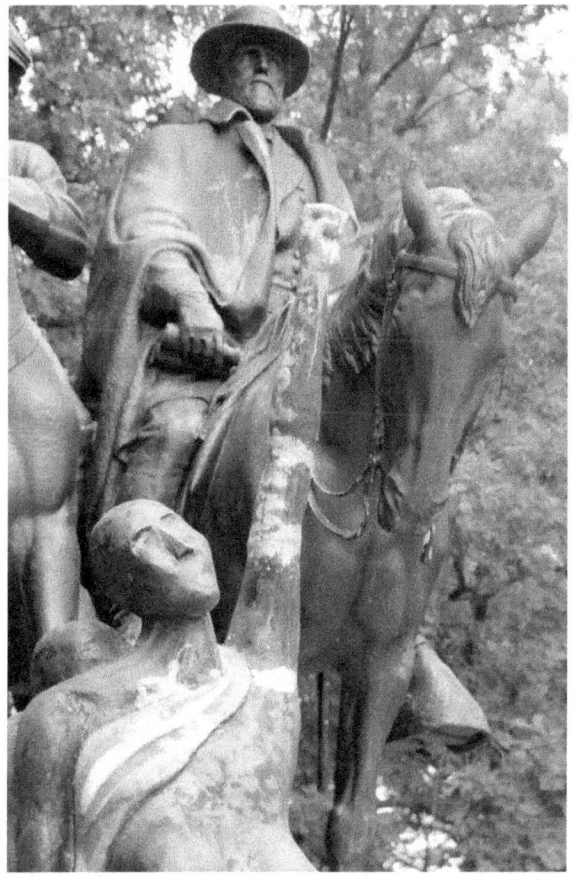

Graffiti on the Jackson and Lee Monument[54]

---

[54] *Protest & Interventions at Confederate Monuments.* 7 Oct. 2015. Photograph. Baltimore, Maryland. Available from: Flickr Commons, Ryan Patterson, https://www.flickr.com/photos/baltimorepublicart/36574207365/in/photolist-XHW15a-XvJPpn-XvJDnP-XDP65E-XDP3PC-XHWnCa-X7TyML-Ws9JuQ-WuprA6-Wupw9z-XHW34a-v4AnvE-XKe5TD-zmzdmG-X5WjYQ-X7TBro-XHWf2t-zmze5A-XDP4aC-WupBj4-Ws9edd-Wupf86-XHWgc4-XHWhy2-Xt3Ls3-WupzMM-Xt3Hhq-WupsXp-XHWjDp-WupxMV-XHVNZV-Wupz5e-XHVQ6c-XHVMjk-XDP4Do-XHW54T-Xt3K41-XHVLgi-X7TDT7-X7TJ6A-Wupbk6-XDP1Pq-XHWkLz-XDP3p9-XHW6V8-XDP36o-Wuphti-XvJN1F-Ws9cYu-X7TKLE/

Graffiti on the Jackson and Lee Monument[55]

[55] *Protest & Interventions at Confederate Monuments.* 7 Oct. 2015. Photograph. Baltimore, Maryland. Available from: Flickr Commons, Ryan Patterson, https://www.flickr.com/photos/baltimorepublicart/35764733723/in/photolist-XHW15a-XvJPpn-XvJDnP-XDP65E-XDP3PC-XHWnCa-X7TyML-Ws9JuQ-WuprA6-Wupw9z-XHW34a-v4AnvE-XKe5TD-zmzdmG-X5WjYQ-X7TBro-XHWf2t-zmze5A-XDP4aC-WupBj4-Ws9edd-Wupf86-XHWgc4-XHWhy2-Xt3Ls3-WupzMM-Xt3Hhq-WupsXp-XHWjDp-WupxMV-XHVNZV-Wupz5e-XHVQ6c-XHVMjk-XDP4Do-XHW54T-Xt3K41-XHVLgi-X7TDT7-X7TJ6A-Wupbk6-XDP1Pq-XHWkLz-XDP3p9-XHW6V8-XDP36o-Wuphti-XvJN1F-Ws9cYu-X7TKLE

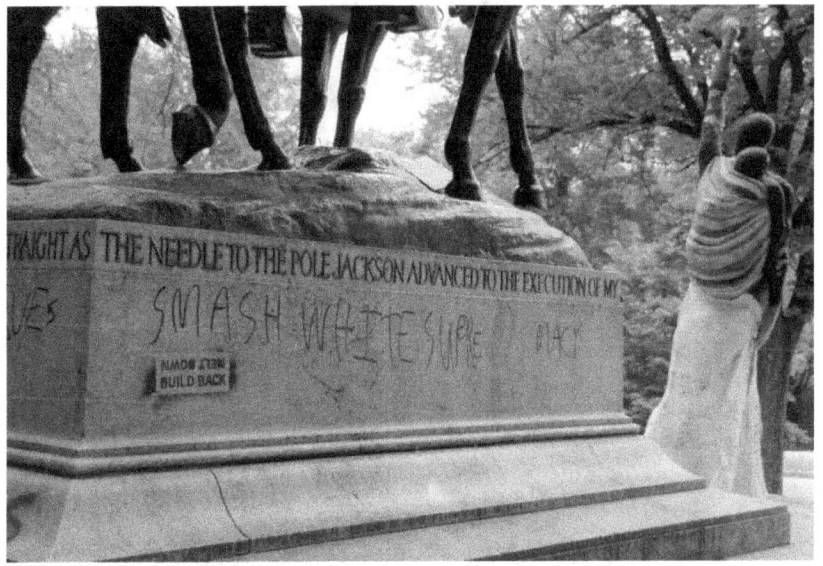

Graffiti on the Jackson and Lee Monument[56]

---

[56] *Protest & Interventions at Confederate Monuments*. 7 Oct. 2015. Photograph. Baltimore, Maryland. Available from: Flickr Commons, Ryan Patterson, https://www.flickr.com/photos/baltimorepublicart/36177607730/in/photolist-WxAVmr-X7TGnq-XM7deH-Wupuzn-XHW15a-WxBiBi-Ay9D4Y-XH36U1-XvJPpn-XwdpyG-Xb5Npq-XM7hkZ-Xwmcnw-XH2zsE-WvijQQ-XM7jAa-XMh9Rv-Ay9Ror-iMba8N-WxCaYk-Xb5N1E-WvikdJ-WxKweg-WvhhsL-WxCcKM-WxBxFv-WxCiC8-XM8hFg-WxCqP2-XyUsDX-XyUMiF-XyV8fe-WxBzqH-Xb5LHu-WvhcZs-Wvih11-XM7t6r-WxCa3x-XyUh24-Xb51tY-XM7mnX-Wvhkc3-XwdpnE-WxBA6F-Bd8R6a-XyUyRr-XM7uRa-XM8FqK-XyV9xV-Wvh4ou

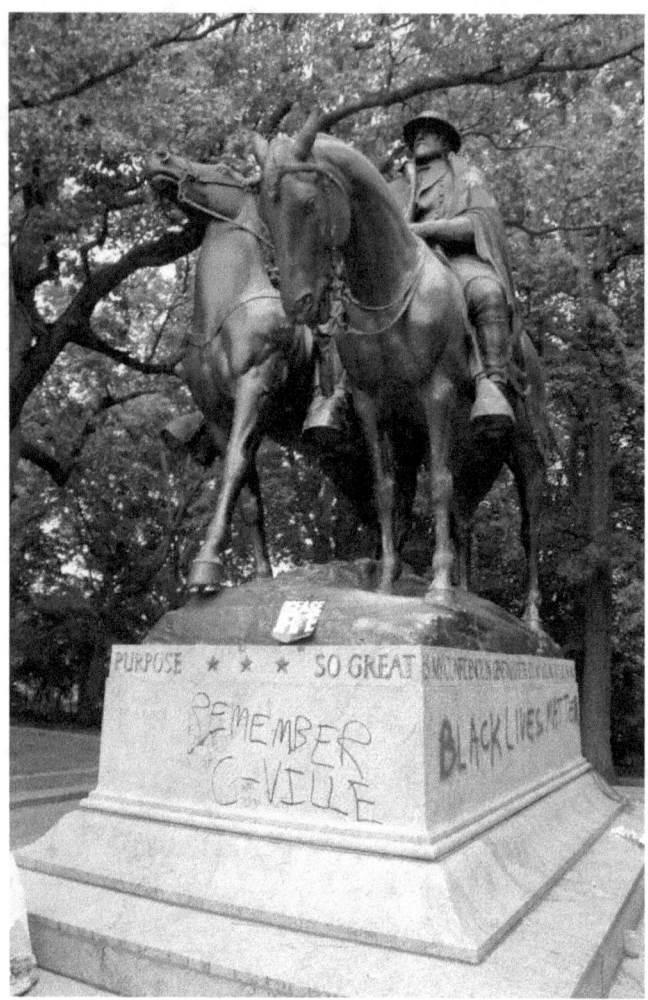

Graffiti on the Jackson and Lee Monument[57]

---

[57] *Protest & Interventions at Confederate Monuments.* 7 Oct. 2015. Photograph. Baltimore, Maryland. Available from: Flickr Commons, Ryan Patterson, https://www.flickr.com/photos/baltimorepublicart/36177591140/in/photolist-XHWmHp-efHGEn-Xwmcnw-Wvh4ou-X7TBro-XHWf2t-WuprA6-XHW34a-XH2zsE-Wupw9z-dzYQDT-UvMTYz-Ws9JuQ-Xz5r5V-p2xSPq-di3J7K-Vj5TwJ-XM7geF-TShmS1-Vce6JL-do2uuV-9szxiz-5UhKAn-84Mm8k-b4M9DF-axdZyh-9d2z2Z-9qHVVe-XWBjkK-XLQSkw-XDP36o-XHWnCa-C443jJ-aDUiTw-bRGWkg-Wupbk6-ba8Hhz-XHVLgi-U1td9d-WktR89-aa2CTr-UvWKbL-8TYMj6-XDP1Pq-WviiJb-WvhPnG-XHWhy2-Xvz6rB-aWX2wg-WSfGhM/

4 NEW ORLEANS, LOUISIANA

New Orleans, a Confederate stronghold, was lost during the battle of New Orleans on April 24, 1862. Taking the stronghold was of utmost importance to the North since it functioned as a port in which the South received supplies from Europe. After breaching the city with a Union naval squadron of forty-three ships, General B.F. Butler, along with his fifteen thousand Union troops, was able to take control of the city for the remainder of the war. Moving up the Mississippi River led to the Union's creation of a desired split in the Confederacy and eventually helped them move towards victory. The permanent loss of New Orleans was considered one of the worst disasters suffered by the Confederacy in the western theatre of the war.[58]

Considering the fact that New Orleans was a part of the Confederacy, it is not surprising that there is an abundance of Confederate statues within the city's borders. During the Reconstruction Era, there remained feelings of attachment to the Confederacy, and these attachments can still be witnessed today. Multiple statues were put up in memory of the Civil War, along with the Confederate Memorial Hall, which is known to be second largest collection of Confederate military artifacts.

A notable individual who was memorialized in New Orleans is

---

[58] "Battle of New Orleans," *Encyclopædia Britannica*, 28 Oct. 2016, www.britannica.com/event/Battle-of-New-Orleans-American-Civil-War-1862.

Jefferson Davis, the first and only president of the Confederacy, who died there in 1889. There once stood a large statue of Davis in the city, before it was removed in response to the Charleston shootings of 2015. Historians believe that the creation of this statue was partially to help reshape Davis's image.[59] Supposedly after Union police arrested him, he tried to escape wearing one of his wife's dresses. The statue was finally removed on May 11, 2017 in the middle of the night. As of October 31, 2017, the statue remains in a city warehouse until a decision can be made regarding where it should reside in the future.

Sean Quigley

---

[59] Tegan Wendland, "With Lee Statue's Removal, Another Battle Of New Orleans Comes To A Close," *National Public Radio*, 20 May 2017, www.npr.org/2017/05/20/529232823/with-lee-statues-removal-another-battle-of-new-orleans-comes-to-a-close.

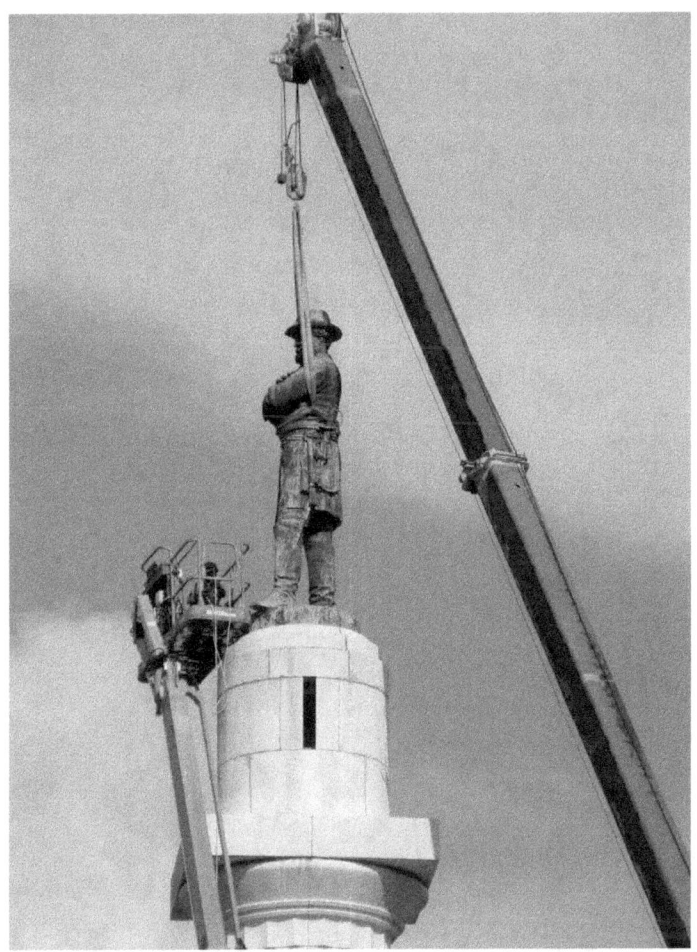

Removal of the Robert E. Lee Statue[60]

[60] *Robert E Lee statue removal.* 19 May 2017. Photograph. Lee Circle, New Orleans, Louisiana. Available from: Wikimedia Commons, Creative Commons Attribution 2.0 Generic license, https://commons.wikimedia.org/wiki/File:General_Lee_Taken_Down_(34726901136).j pg

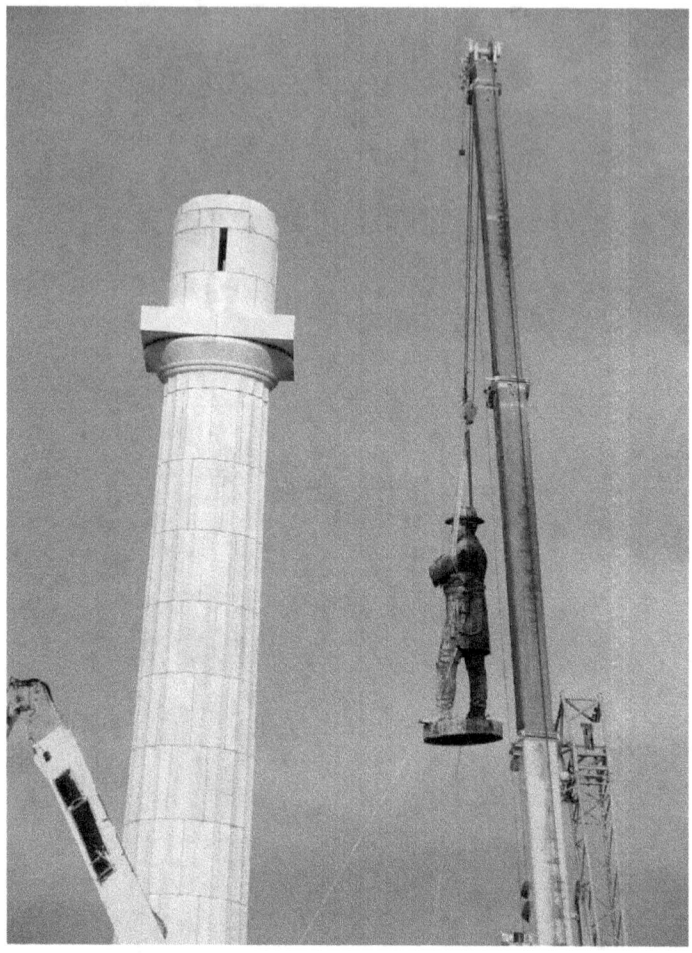

The Remaining Empty Pedestal Following the Removal of the
Robert E. Lee Statue[61]

---

[61] *Robert E Lee statue removed from column.* 19 May 2017. Photograph. Lee
Circle, New Orleans, Louisiana. Available from: Wikimedia Commons,
https://upload.wikimedia.org/wikipedia/commons/2/2e/Robert_E_Lee_statue_removed
_from_column_New_Orleans_19_May_2017_12.jpg

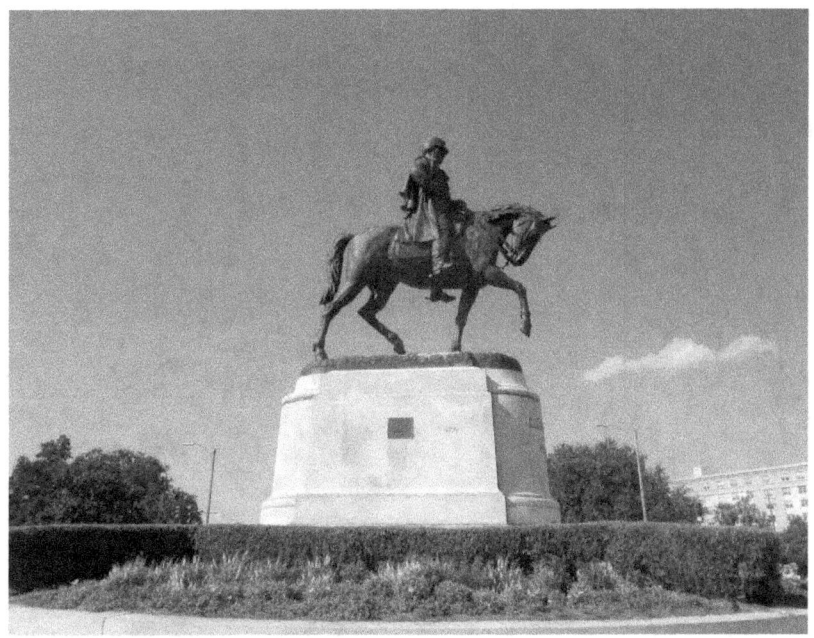

Statue of P.G.T. Beauregard[62]

---

[62] Alexander Doyle. *General Beauregard Equestrian Statue.* 1915. Statue. New Orleans, Louisiana. Available from: Wikimedia Commons, https://upload.wikimedia.org/wikipedia/commons/8/86/Beauregard_Statue_July_2015.jpg

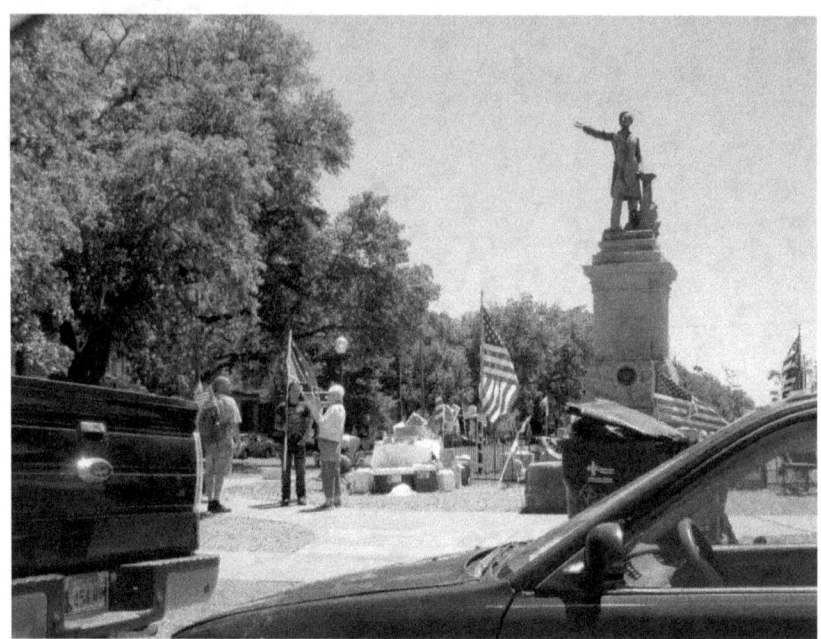

Supporters Around the Jefferson Davis Statue[63]

[63] Edward Virginius Valentine. *Jefferson Davis Monument*. 1911. Statue. New Orleans, Louisiana Available from: Wikimedia Commons, https://upload.wikimedia.org/wikipedia/commons/5/5b/Worshiping_the_Traitor_Davis _Idol.jpg

5 DURHAM, NORTH CAROLINA

Durham was a very significant site in the Civil War because it was the location of the largest troop surrender in 1865, the surrender which effectively ended the war.[64] In Durham, Generals Sherman and Johnston met at a common place between their two armies to draft a proposal for a war-ending treaty. This common place was a farm owned by James and Nancy Bennett, which is heavily trafficked by visitors who wish to learn more about the conclusion of the Civil War. Today, the city of Durham contains some of the world's largest tobacco-producing industries and is a Civil War tourist hotspot.

In reaction to the Charleston shootings, protests have emerged in Durham and several Confederate monuments have been removed. One statue to be removed out of protest is a Confederate soldier monument which was located outside of the Durham courthouse in the city's downtown area. Inscribed on the monument was "In memory of the boys who wore gray".[65]

The statue depicts a fallen soldier which represents the Confederacy's cause as a whole. Many people in Durham had relatives who fought in the Civil War, so it is understandable why

---

[64] "Durham's Role in the Civil War," *Civil War History*, www.durham-nc.com/things-to-do/features/civil-war-history/.

[65] Maggie Astor, "Protesters in Durham Topple a Confederate Monument," *The New York Times*, 14 Aug. 2017, www.nytimes.com/2017/08/14/us/protesters-in-durham-topple-a-confederate-monument.html.

memorials would be placed in the city following the war's conclusion. That being said, the context of the statue has changed along with generational changes defining the people that inhabit Durham. While it once may have served as a memorial to people whose lives were lost, this statue is now believed to embody the racist philosophies of a growing neo-nazi population within the United States.

The placement of this statue was clearly a form of intimidation aimed at people of color post-Civil War. Erecting a statue in memory of the Confederacy outside of a courthouse could send the message that racism exists within the legal system.

Sean Quigley

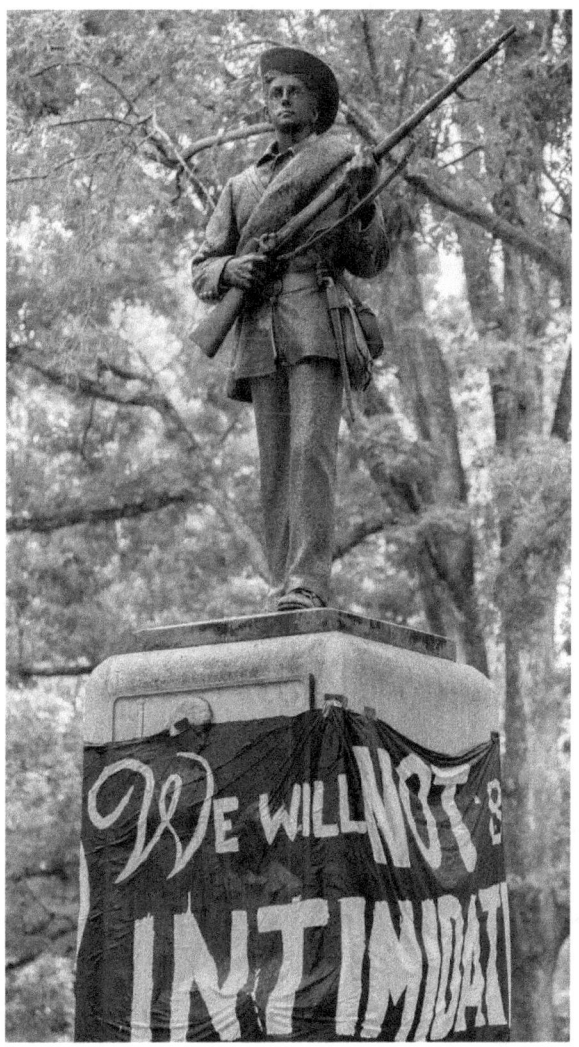

Silent Sam on the UNC Chapel Hill Campus[66]

---

[66] *Protests against the statue of Silent Sam.* 23 Aug. 2017. Photograph. University of North Carolina at Chapel Hill. Available from: Wikimedia Commons, Martin J. Kraft, Free licence CC BY-SA 3.0, https://commons.wikimedia.org/wiki/File:MJK49379_Silent_Sam.jpg

6 NEW YORK, NEW YORK

New York City was a hub of activity during the Civil War. Politically, it was democratic and pro-war. However, the city also had strong economic ties to the South. For this reason, there were a number of businessmen and wealthy individuals who adamantly opposed the war. New York City was an extremely important center for recruiting and training soldiers to fight against the South. It is estimated that the city gathered and sent out about one hundred thousand New York soldiers during the war.[67]

In an overwhelmingly democratic northern city, it is surprising to many that there are a few Confederate monuments in the city. In the week after the recent events in Charlottesville, New York City mayor, Bill de Blasio, announced a "90-day review of all symbols of hate on city property".[68]

The Bronx Community College contains an old and renowned Hall of Fame for Great Americans. There are almost one hundred bronze busts of notable Americans, who were chosen through a public voting process and accepted by a committee, lining this hall. Two of these busts are of Confederate Generals Robert E. Lee and

---

[67] "New York City in the American Civil War," *Wikipedia*, 13 Nov. 2017, en.wikipedia.org/wiki/New_York_City_in_the_American_Civil_War.

[68] Amy Plitt, "De Blasio Says NYC Will Review 'Symbols of Hate' on City Property," *Curbed New York*, 17 Aug. 2017, ny.curbed.com/2017/8/17/16162118/nyc-bill-de-blasio-monuments-review.

Stonewall Jackson. They were added after an extensive letter writing campaign led by the United Daughters of the Confederacy and are believed to have been approved as additions in an attempt to heal the split between the North and the South. The United Daughters of the Confederacy funded the construction of these busts, that of Lee in 1923 and that of Jackson in 1957, and their installation.[69]

After the events in Charlottesville, the existence of these busts became a concern for many New Yorkers. The population of the Bronx Community College is predominantly black and Latino, and the presence of pro-slavery figures is problematic. Bronx Borough President, Ruben Diaz Jr., stated that these busts "should not stay in the Bronx any longer" and proposed sending the busts to the New York State Military Museum. Governor Cuomo also condemned the statues, announcing that "New York stands against racism".[70] On August 18th, 2017, the statues were both removed from the hall and have not yet been relocated.

On August 16, two days earlier, two plaques in Brooklyn commemorating Robert E. Lee were removed. These plaques were installed in 1912, also by the United Daughters of the Confederacy, next to a maple tree that Lee planted while he was stationed at nearby Fort Hamilton. One plaque described the origin of the tree and recognized the efforts of the United Daughters of the Confederacy while the other described the replacement of the tree after the death of the original.[71] Church officials encouraged the

---

[69] JB Nicholas, "Robert E. Lee & Stonewall Jackson Are Part Of Bronx Community College's 'Hall Of Fame'," *Gothamist*, 16 Aug. 2017, gothamist.com/2017/08/16/robert_e_lee_stonewall_jackson_bron.php#photo-1.

[70] Aaron Short, "From the Bronx to Brooklyn, Confederate Symbols Come Down Across New York City," *Hyperallergic*, 22 Aug. 2017, hyperallergic.com/397022/confederate-symbols-removed-nyc/.

[71] Caroline Spivack, "Robert E. Lee Memorial Removed From Tree at Fort Hamilton Church," *DNA Info New York*, 16 Aug. 2017, www.dnainfo.com/new-york/20170816/fort-hamilton/robert-e-lee-memorial-church-of-the-generals-st-johns-episcopal-church.

removal of the tree and plaques, located on the grounds of St. John's Episcopal Church. After Charlottesville, Bishop Lawrence Provenzano, of the Episcopal Diocese of Long Island, explained that "it became very clear to all of us that this reminder of the oppressive nature of a time in our history that really needs to be righted, should be removed from the church property".[72]

One very controversial statue that has not yet been removed is located in Central Park. It is a prominent sculpture commemorating the achievements of "the father of modern gynecology", Dr. J. Marion Sims. While he made a number of important discoveries, he also infamously performed experiments on enslaved black women. While not directly related to the Confederacy, Sims' story has been included in the debate because it involves the issue of slavery. On August 26th, the word "racist" was spray painted on the statue in big red letters.[73] It has since been cleaned of any traces of vandalism and remains in Central Park.

Nicky Paulson

---

[72] Tea Kvetenadze and Lia Eustachewich, "Robert E. Lee Plaque Removed from Brooklyn Church," *New York Post*, 16 Aug. 2017, nypost.com/2017/08/16/robert-e-lee-plaque-removed-from-church-property/.

[73] Ellen Moynihan and Rich Schapiro, "Vandal Defaces NYC Statue of Doctor Who Experimented on Slaves," *New York Daily News*, 26 Aug. 2017, www.nydailynews.com/new-york/manhattan/vandal-defaces-nyc-statue-doctor-experimented-slaves-article-1.3445268.

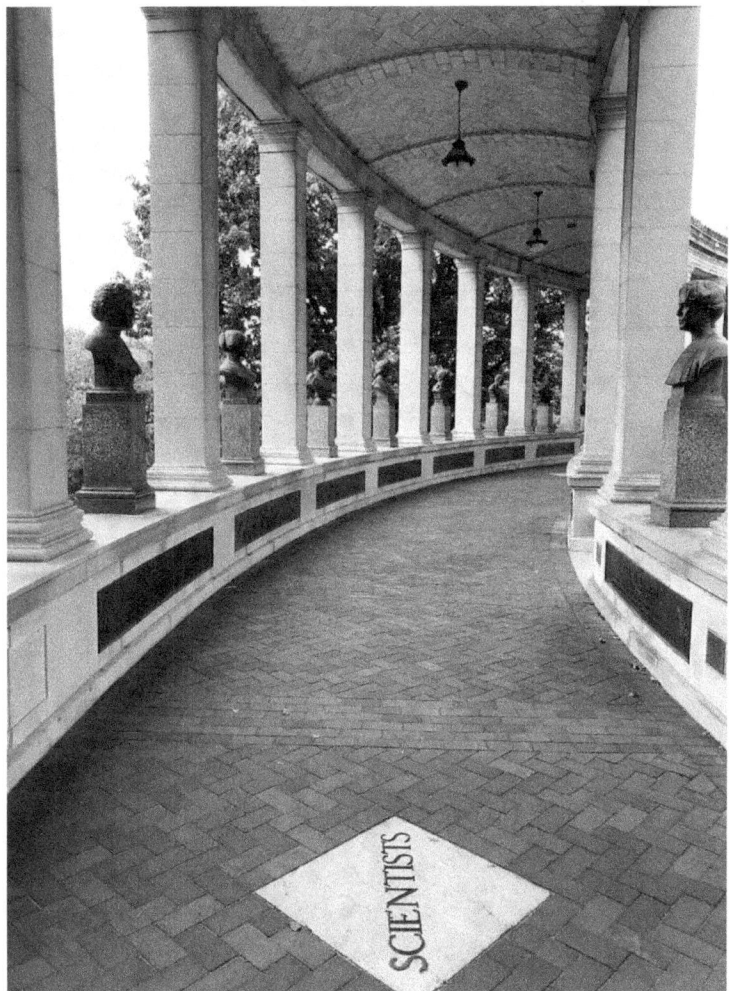

Hall of Fame at Bronx Community College[74]

[74] *Recently removed are the heads of Confederates Robert E Lee and Stonewall Jackson.* 15 Oct. 2017. Photograph. Hall of Fame Bronx Community College, New York. Available from: Wikimedia Commons, Creative Commons Attribution-Share Alike 4.0 International license, https://commons.wikimedia.org/wiki/File:A_walk_in_the_hall_of_fame.jpg

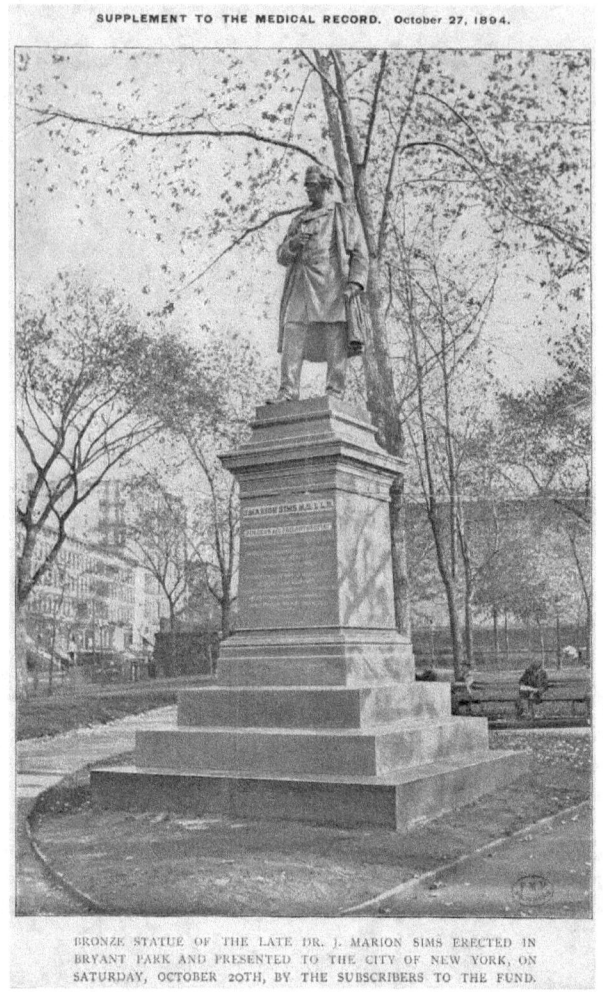

SUPPLEMENT TO THE MEDICAL RECORD. October 27, 1894.

BRONZE STATUE OF THE LATE DR. J. MARION SIMS ERECTED IN
BRYANT PARK AND PRESENTED TO THE CITY OF NEW YORK, ON
SATURDAY, OCTOBER 20TH, BY THE SUBSCRIBERS TO THE FUND.

Statue of Marion Sims in Bryant Park, Manhattan[75]

[75] Ferdinand von Miller II. *Dr. J. Marion Sims*. 20 Oct. 1894. Bronze statue. Bryant Park, Manhattan, New York. Available from: Wikimedia Commons, *Licence Ouverte*, https://commons.wikimedia.org/wiki/File:Bronze_statue_of_the_late_Dr_J._Marion_Si ms_erected_in_Bryant_Park_and_CIPB0963.jpg

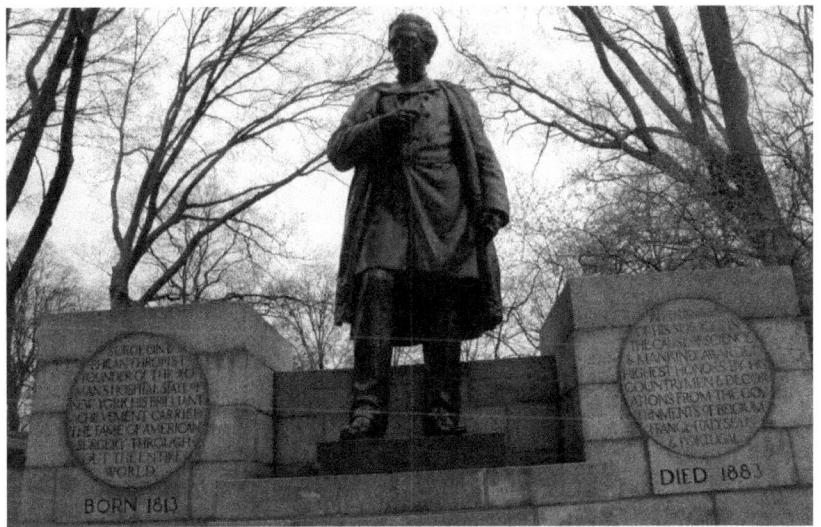

Statue of Marion Sims in Bryant Park, Manhattan[76]

---

[76] Ferdinand von Miller II. *J. Marion Sims Monument*. 20 Oct. 1894. Bronze Statue. Bryant Park, Manhattan, New York. Available from: Flickr Commons, Attribution-Share Alike 2.0 Generic license, https://www.flickr.com/photos/nauright/5660048424/in/photolist-9CaecN-9CafjG-VGP5Bu/

7 MADISON, WISCONSIN

Although far from the South, Madison had an active role in the Civil War. Camp Randall, the football stadium at which the University of Wisconsin Badgers play, was first an important training camp for Union soldiers. Thousands of Union soldiers passed through Camp Randall, evident through the presence of numerous and extravagant monuments in its vicinity. However, less known is the fact that Camp Randall also contained a prisoner of war camp for captured Confederate soldiers.[77] One hundred and forty of these soldiers died because of disease, wounds, or malnutrition while held in Madison. As a result, they are buried near Camp Randall in a section of Forest Hills Cemetery called the Confederate Rest. The Confederate Rest is the northernmost Confederate cemetery. One hundred ten of the deceased are from the first Alabama Infantry, while the rest are from Arkansas, Tennessee, Louisiana, and Mississippi.[78]

After the war ended, the fallen Confederate soldiers were eventually forgotten. The grass became overgrown and the wooden headboards marking the graves started to deteriorate. Then, in 1868, a woman named Alice Waterman moved to Madison. She was born in the South but spent most of her life in the North. Waterman had no

---

[77] "Confederate Prisoners at Camp Randall as Seen in Newspaper Articles," *Wisconsin Historical Society*, 3 Oct. 2012, www.wisconsinhistory.org/Records/Article/CS3408.

[78] Mark, "The Confederate Cemetery in Madison, Wisconsin," *Iron Brigader*, 15 June 2015, ironbrigader.com/2015/06/15/confederate-cemetery-madison-wisconsin/.

personal connection to any of the buried Confederates, but she believed that their graves should be better cared for and respected. Spending her own time and money, she cleaned the overgrowth, replaced the headboards, and erected a small fence around the area.[79] She eventually caught the attention of former Union generals, Lucius Fairchild and C.C. Washburn, who both became Wisconsin governors. Washburn and Fairchild helped ensure the maintenance of the Confederate Rest and even led trips there on Memorial Day for people to pay their respects.

In 1897, Alice Waterman passed away and was buried in front of the Confederate graves for which she had spent so much time caring. As recorded on her grave's headstone, she referred to these deceased Confederates as "her boys".

After the recent events in Charlottesville regarding Confederate statues and memorials, Madisonians reconsidered two monuments placed next to the Confederate graves. The first is simply a plaque that describes who is buried and how they were captured. It was privately funded and installed in 1981. However, the language of this plaque was seen as problematic by many, including Madison mayor, Paul Soglin. The plaque refers to the buried soldiers as "unsung heroes" who were considered to be "valiant." Soglin announced his concern that this plaque "speak[s] in glowing terms about the historic efforts of the Confederacy." As a result, this plaque was removed in August of 2017 and will be replaced with one that solely lists the names of the dead.[80] He insisted that "there is no disrespect to the dead with the removal of the plaque and stone."

---

[79] Jessie Beckett, "Camp Randall, Alice Waterman, and the Culture of Death: Madison's Steps to Reconnection," *Minds at UW*, 13 May 2015, minds.wisconsin.edu/handle/1793/72872.

[80] Logan Wroge, "Madison Mayor Paul Soglin Orders Removal of Confederate Monuments at Forest Hill Cemetery," *Wisconsin State Journal*, 18 Aug. 2017, host.madison.com/wsj/news/local/madison-mayor-paul-soglin-orders-removal-of-confederate-monuments-at/article_0cd509e6-3b6b-56ab-b05c-c693d84de05d.html.

The second object of focus is a much larger stone monument. This one was erected in 1931 by the Daughters of the Confederacy and has received even more criticism from Soglin. He insisted that it "is not a Civil War monument" because it was installed sixty years after the war. Instead he believes it to be a "despicable fixture honoring slavery, sedition and oppression." He refers to the monument as propaganda paid for by a "racist organization" to promote a new form of racism. This monument has not yet been dealt with but will likely either be removed or supplemented by an additional plaque that would describe how the Daughters of the Confederacy have and continue to "spread lies about slavery".[81]

Nicky Paulson

---

[81] James B. Nelson, "Madison Mayor Paul Soglin Orders Removal of Two Confederate Memorials from Cemetery," *Milwaukee Journal Sentinel*, 17 Aug. 2017, www.jsonline.com/story/news/2017/08/17/madison-mayor-paul-soglin-orders-removal-two-confederate-memorials-cemetery/576266001/.

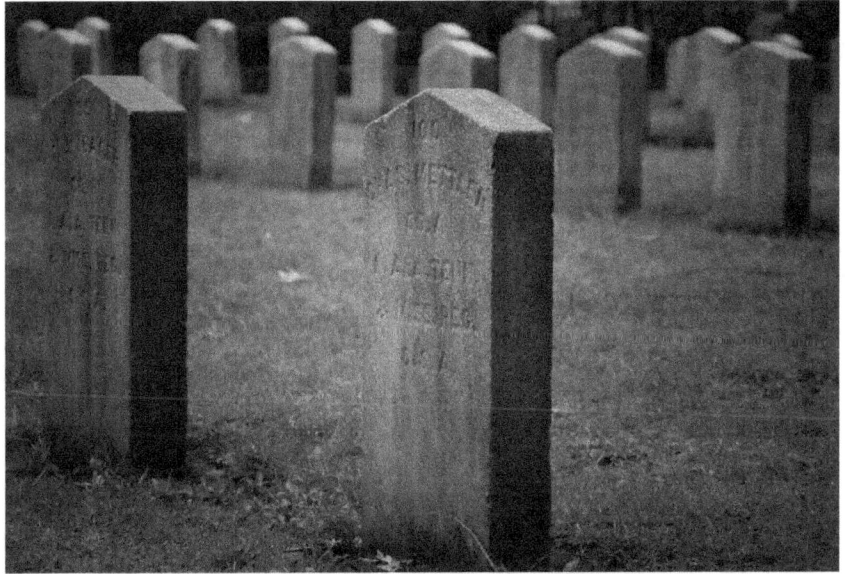

Confederate Graves in Forest Hills Cemetery[82]

[82] *Confederate graves at Forest Hill Cemetery*. 25 April 2011. Photograph. Madison, Wisconsin. Available from: Wikimedia Commons, Creative Commons Attribution-Share Alike 3.0 Unported license, https://upload.wikimedia.org/wikipedia/commons/f/f3/Confederate_graves_at_Forest_Hill _Cemetery%2C_Madison%2C_Wisconsin_4-27-2011_023.jpg

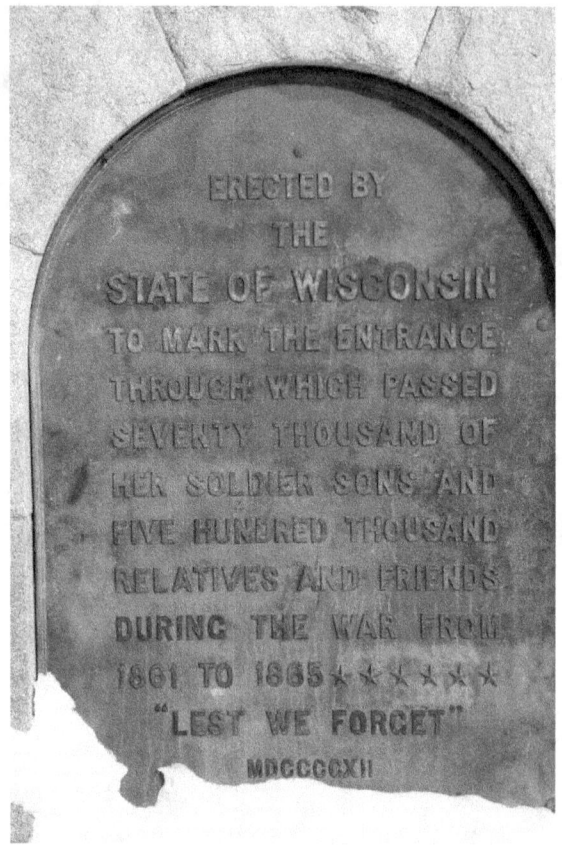

Plaque in the archway of Camp Randall[83]

[83] *Camp Randall Archway Plaque.* Madison, Wisconsin. Available from: Flickr Commons, Jeff Christiansen, Attribution-Share Alike 2.0 Generic license, https://www.flickr.com/photos/jeffchristiansen/2263526633/in/photolist-4s2aBg-oQvLHr-6yRfLK-pPPqNg-71KgBd-71FfBz-71KfWy-71KgjU-4s2aaZ-aELXrc-ddDGdf-jeHFx9-ddDQBV-mXHnNv-ietpvH-aksnYo-eZnk5j-eZb39X-gKDoAL-eZno2b-o5qmYh-ddDTbD-i9RgRb-8tSS4r-4x1nSk-9epyZF-5safsG-k21rA-7c3TJN-4s2akM-4s6cE7-7BbiQp-j2uNMK-4s6diQ-fvNah4-4s6crC-7BfmGd-7BCxFk-7bWTh6-5Tf86-7DE1uQ-7Bffy7-iDh5wP-g48TZ4-u79R7-8Bwy85-g3SeDB-222hp-b6dAGT-b6dACV

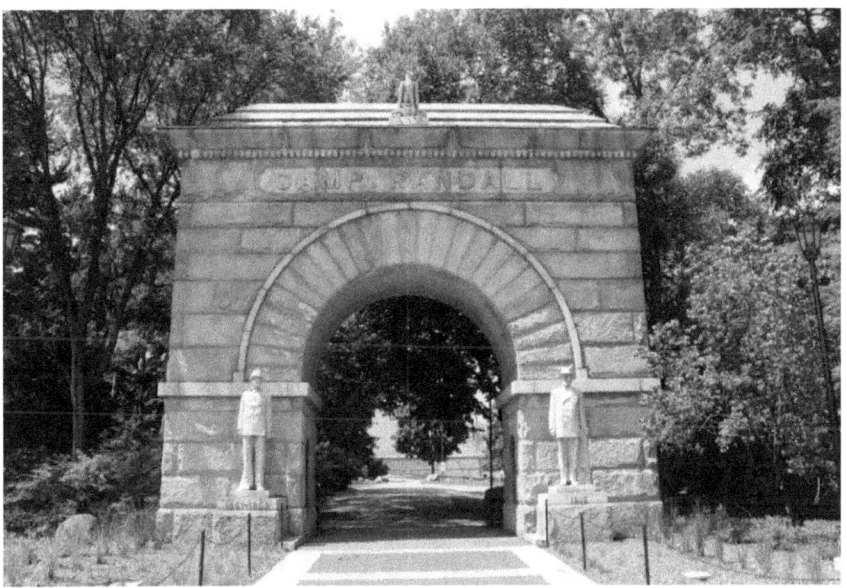

Gateway to Camp Randall Stadium[84]

[84] Lew F. Porter. *Camp Randall Memorial Arch*. 1912. Madison, Wisconsin. Available from: Flickr Commons, Jason Dean, Attribution-Share Alike 2.0 Generic license, https://www.flickr.com/photos/thed34n/4909966767/in/photolist-8tSS4r-4x1nSk-9epyZE-5safsG-k21rA-7c3TJN-4s2akM-4s6cE7-7BbiQp-j2uNMK-4s6diQ-fvNah4-4s6crC-7BfmGd-7BCxFk-7bWTh6-5Tf86-7DE1uQ-7Bffy7-iDh5wP-g48TZ4-u79R7-8Bwy85-g3SeDB-222hp-b6dAGT-b6dACV-qwmsa-3bpwmB-4ZsLi-5VP8E-qwmt7-7bZWEa-g48W6E-aqGWjo-g49ucR-ddDBz6-ddDFor-aEQQaY-jbsCnC-eZnogU-RzWm3v-4aGTyz-eW13Qh-eZb2mB-depvgd-meGUNR-7XAxqn-pG3Vbj-3bufP3

8 ARGUMENTS TO KEEP THE STATUES

Following the August 12, 2017 anti-White Nationalist Rally in Charlottesville, Virginia,, the Charlottesville City Council unanimously voted to cover statues of Robert E. Lee and Thomas Jonathan "Stonewall" Jackson as a way of mourning the loss of Heather Heyer, Virginia State Police Lieutenant Cullen, and Trooper-Pilot Berke M.M. Bates, all of whom lose their lives during the rally. Judge Richard Moore of the Charlottesville Circuit Court placed a temporary injunction to protect both statues from removal until November 2, 2017.[85]

Lawyers involved in the protection of the statues filed their lawsuit against the city's effort to remove the statues on March 20, 2017. Their goal was to stop the Charlottesville City Council from removing the Lee statue. The lawsuit claimed that the "councilors had acted beyond their authority and violated a state law that prohibits removing monuments or memorials to war veterans".[86] Despite the pushback from locals, Charlottesville City Council unanimously voted on September 5, 2017

---

[85] John Early, "Charlottesville Judge Rules Confederate Statue Shrouds Remain," *NBC 29*, 4 Oct. 2017, www.nbc29.com/story/36521561/circuit-court-confederate-statues-10-04-2017.

[86] Ibid

to remove the Jackson statue.[87]

The Robert E. Lee statue that is located in Emancipation Park, formerly Lee Park, was conceived by Henry M. Shrady, completed by Leo Lentelli, and presented by Paul Goodloe McIntire in 1924. McIntire also donated the land on which the park is located to the city in 1917, in memory of his parents, intending for the land to be used as a public park. McIntire presented this site to the city of Charlottesville to "erect thereon a statue of General Robert E. Lee and present said property to the City as a memorial to his parents." On behalf of Paul McIntire, Dr. Henry Louis Smith, President of Washington and Lee University, presented the sculpture to Charlottesville, making the statute the property of the city.[88]

McIntire was Charlottesville's biggest benefactor. He donated the land for Emancipation Park on behalf of whites, and Washington Park, named after Booker T. Washington, on behalf of blacks, attempting to create balance. The donation of the Lee statue was part of the early 20th century's City Beautiful Movement, which aimed to create well-designed and attractive public spaces. Many saw the statue as McIntire's gift as a war memorial.[89] However, according to the trial's judge, there is insufficient information to claim that the Lee statue is a war memorial.[90]

In Charlottesville during August of 2017, Allen Armentrout, a man from North Carolina, guarded the Lee statue. He dressed in a Confederate soldier's uniform, carried a Confederate flag, and held an assault rifle at the statue. Armentrout did not agree with the violence or

---

[87] Ibid

[88] "Emancipation Park (Formerly Known as Lee Park)," *City of Charlottesville*, www.charlottesville.org/departments-and-services/departments-h-z/parks-recreation-/parks-trails/city-parks/emancipation-park-formerly-known-as-lee-park.

[89] Lisa Provence, "Paul Goodloe McIntire: Goodwill to All Men?" *C-Ville*, 30 Mar. 2016, www.c-ville.com/paul-goodloe-mcintire-goodwill-men/#.Wh30PbaZMkh.

[90] John Early, "Charlottesville Judge Rules Confederate Statue Shrouds Remain," *NBC 29*, 4 Oct. 2017, www.nbc29.com/story/36521561/circuit-court-confederate-statues-10-04-2017.

the different perspectives presented by those passionate about the issues surrounding the Confederate statues. He said "it hurts my heart that people come out here and misappropriate Robert E. Lee and the Confederate flag for their personal agendas. I'm out here to honor my ancestors and honor the men who died under the command of Robert E. Lee, and I think me being out here shows that I hope to accomplish the fact that the world can see that there's non-racist pro-Confederate people out there that love freedom and independence".[91]

In the state of North Carolina, there are legal bindings and requirements that prevent Confederate statues, many of which are public property, from being removed and relocated to different locations. According to Chapter 100 G.S. 100-2.1, Protection of Monuments, Memorials, and Works of Art, "any monument, memorial, or work of art owned by the State may not be removed, relocated, or altered in any way without the approval of the North Carolina Historical Commission." There are limitations on the removal of objects of remembrance, which are legally defined as "a monument, memorial, plaque, statue, marker, or display of a permanent character that commemorates an event, a person, or military service that is part of North Carolina's history." In clause B, it states, "an object on public property may not be permanently removed and may only be relocated, whether temporarily or permanently", "an object of remembrance that is permanently relocated shall be relocated to a site of similar prominence, honor, visibility, availability, and access", and "an object of remembrance may not be relocated to a museum, cemetery, or mausoleum unless it was originally placed at such a location." An object of remembrance may be relocated if "appropriate measures are required by the State or a political subdivision of the State to preserve the object" or if relocation is "necessary for construction, renovation, or reconfiguration of buildings, open spaces, parking or transportation projects." The exceptions to this

---

[91] Aaron Moody, "NC Man Guarding Robert E. Lee Statue: 'There's Non-Racist, pro-Confederate People out There'," *The News & Observer*, 16 Aug. 2017, www.newsobserver.com/news/local/article167504092.html.

rule include highway markers, "[objects] of remembrance owned by a private party that [are] located on public property and that [are] the subject of legal agreement between the private party and the State of political subdivision of the State governing the removal or relocation of the [objects]," and "[objects] of remembrance for which a building inspector or similar official has determined [pose] a threat to public safety because of unsafe or dangerous condition".[92]

Michael Chan

Preserve Southern Pride

As tensions rose around the potential removal of the Confederate statues, protesters in support of keeping the monuments argue that the monuments commemorate Southern history and pride. For example, sixty-eight-year-old Virginian, David Lawler, was not born when the monuments were erected. He is in support of keeping the monuments up, because "they were put up to honor men that were very honorable and totally committed to duty".[93] Several of the monuments describe the bodies as heroes and saviors on markers "dedicated to the immortal spirit of the Confederate Cause, and to those men and women who gave so much to save what they considered so dear".[94] In addition to supporting Southern history, honoring those who fought during the Civil War justified keeping the monuments as they stand.

A man sat in front of a Virginia Robert E. Lee statue in summer 2017. When NPR's Code Switch asked what he was doing, he said that he was protecting "an American veteran, by which he meant Robert E.

---

[92] North Carolina § 100-2.1, Protection of monuments, memorials, and works of art, (2015).

[93] Ned Oliver, "RTD-CNU Poll: Majority of Richmond Residents Oppose Removing Confederate Statues, Support Adding Historical Context," *Richmond Times-Dispatch*, 4 Oct. 2017, www.richmond.com/news/local/city-of-richmond/poll-percent-of-richmond-city-residents-oppose-removing-confederate-statues/article_f3f157a6-5e73-54cf-bbee-5d587ea604bd.html.

[94] Ibid

Lee. And he said that most people didn't know that Lee was in the U.S. military".[95]

The statues are defended with claims that the statues inherit and promote Southern heritage, not white supremacy. B Frank Earnest, a published writer in the Richmond-Times Dispatch, believes that the statues are being taken out of context, and wants to keep the statues as they are:

> But Southern heritage is not slavery to us. It is the lifestyle that we have in the South that's different. And everybody to this days says, you know, we do things at a slower pace. We talk differently. We eat different foods. It is. It's a culture just like the black culture or any other culture. And these men to us are men who defended that culture and that heritage, not men who fought to keep slavery.[96]

Earnest later says that slavery is not a part of Southern heritage. It was "more fuel on the already burning fire [...] But the fire was already there before you threw more fuel onto it".[97] In contrast to Southern pride, preserving the darker side of Southern history is another argument for keeping the statues in their original location.

Michael Chan

Remember History

In May 2017, former Secretary of State Condoleezza Rice argued that the Confederate statues should remain standing because they function as a reminder of past events that should not be repeated. Rice believes Americans must remember who these monuments depict and

---

[95] "What Our Monuments (Don't) Teach Us about Remembering the Past," *Code Switch*, National Public Radio, 23 Aug. 2017, www.npr.org/templates/transcript/transcript.php?storyId=545548965.

[96] Ibid

[97] Ibid

what they stood for, as a way to recognize why they are no longer relevant.

> Nobody is alive today who remembers the Civil War, but by looking at [the monuments], you can trigger what it meant and what it was like. You don't have to honor the purposes of people whose history now shows that they were on the other side of history, but you better be able to remind people.[98]

Her position is not unique. Other prominent individuals in American politics believe that the presence of statues in public spaces act as an essential reminder of the country's history. After the riot in Charlottesville, Virginia, President Donald Trump stated that the monuments are an educational tool. "You can't change history, but you can learn from it," he said in a tweet.[99] The vice president agrees with President Trump. Mike Pence told Ainsley Earhardt of "Fox & Friends" that he believes it is important to acknowledge the events of the past and for the country to continue to build on the progress that has been made since the Civil War. "I'm someone who believes in more monuments, not less monuments," he said. "What we ought to do is we ought to remember our history."[100]

Not only are individuals in government in defense of the monuments, but many different Southern groups are also showing their support. The United Daughters of the Confederacy is the group

---

[98] Frank Camp, "Four Perspectives On Removing Confederate Monuments," *The Daily Wire*, 15 Aug. 2017, http://www.dailywire.com/news/19768/four-perspectives-removing-confederate-monuments-frank-camp

[99] David Jackson, "President Trump Defends Confederate Monuments: 'You Can't Change History'," *Milwaukee Journal Sentinel*, 17 Aug. 2017, https://www.usatoday.com/story/news/politics/2017/08/17/trump-attacks-two-republican-senators-criticizing-his-charlottesville-response/575411001/

[100] Paul Waldman, "The Lie of Maintaining Confederate Monuments in the Name of 'History'," *The Washington Post*, 22 Aug. 2017, www.washingtonpost.com/blogs/plum-line/wp/2017/08/22/the-lie-of-maintaining-confederate-monuments-in-the-name-of-history/?utm_term=.19d749d9bc05.

behind the construction of the majority of the South's 718 monuments and the monuments located in New York.[101] Since its founding in 1894, the United Daughters of the Confederacy (UDC) has been a strong proponent of preserving the region's history. After refusing to speak for over a week after the protests in Charlottesville, the UDC finally released a statement on August 21, 2017:

> It is our sincere wish that our great nation and its citizens will continue to let its fellow Americans, the descendants of Confederate soldiers, honor the memory of their ancestors [....] Join us in denouncing hate groups and affirming that Confederate memorial statues and monuments are part of our shared American history and should remain in place.[102]

The UDC's stance is not dissimilar to that of other Southern groups who are currently erecting new monuments, despite the removals that are taking place in cities across the country.

In September 2017, David Coggin dedicated his Confederate Veterans Memorial Park in Brantley, Alabama to Confederate soldiers who died during the Civil War. "What I want to get across is how much the South suffered, not only through the war but after the war, during the Reconstruction years," Coggins said.[103]

A Sons of Confederate Veterans unit in South Carolina recently dedicated a granite memorial to private land where Civil War re-enactments occur annually. Danny Francis, the commander of the

---

[101] Max Kutner, "As Confederate Statues Fall, the Group Behind Most of Them Stays Quiet," *Newsweek*, 25 Aug. 2017, http://www.newsweek.com/united-daughters-confederacy-statues-monuments-udc-653103.

[102] Ibid

[103] Associated Press, "Amid Outcry over Confederate Memorials, New Ones Are Going Up," *Los Angeles Times*, 30 Sept. 2017, http://www.latimes.com/nation/nationnow/la-na-confederate-memorials-20170930-story.html.

group, defended the memorial by saying it's "not trying to oppress anyone - we're just historians."[104]

In Dahlonega, Georgia, a new memorial was just erected on Courthouse Hill. The memorial is sponsored by the Blue Ridge Sons of Confederate Veterans Camp 1860. Tim Ragland, the commander of the group, states that the organization's mission "is to protect and preserve the true history of the South and the Confederacy."[105]

Art Historians

Many art historians have also joined the debate about what should be done with the Confederate monuments. The consensus among most scholars is that the statues should be kept, but moved.

As determined by professionals in the field, most of the statues have no artistic value, but there are a few exceptions.[106] Many have been classified as not being art because they were mass-produced, quickly and sloppily. The majority of monuments were funded and commissioned by city or state governments, not by artists. "The monuments were not intended as public art...they are political statements whose meaning was clearly understood by their targets," says the Society of Architectural Historians.[107] Artist Adam Pendleton agrees with this statement. The Confederate monuments "are not works of art, they're propaganda," he says. "To equate them with how a work of art exists in the world is a false equation".[108]

---

[104] Ibid

[105] Ibid

[106] Dell Upton, "Confederate Monuments and Civic Values in the Wake of Charlottesville," *Society of Architectural Historians Blog*, 13 Sept. 2017, http://www.sah.org/publications-and-research/sah-blog/sah-blog/2017/09/13/confederate-monuments-and-civic-values-in-the-wake-of-charlottesville.

[107] Ibid

[108] Robin Pogrebin and Sopan Deb, "Trump Aside, Artists and Preservationists Debate the Rush to Topple Statues," *The New York Times*, 18 Aug. 2017, https://www.nytimes.com/2017/08/18/arts/design/confederate-statues-artists-

Although most of the monuments are not viewed as art, many art historians and critics believe the statues should still be preserved rather than destroyed. Holland Cotter, co-chief art critic at *The New York Times,* believes the Confederate monuments should be moved to museums because:

> When you find yourself at a crime scene, you don't destroy evidence. You preserve it for the prosecution. In the case of images like this, the prosecutor is history, and the trial may be a long one, stretching far into the future, with many witnesses called. Rush to judgment and drastic action should be resisted.[109]

However, there are a few monuments that historians do value as art. The statue of Stonewall Jackson in Charlottesville was erected by renowned sculptor Charles Keck, and the statue of Robert E. Lee in Richmond was crafted by the acclaimed sculptor Jean-Antoine Merci.[110] Hollis Robbins, a humanities professor at Johns Hopkins University, argues that the equestrian statue of Generals Lee and Jackson by Laura Gardin Fraser is also a work of art. "Artwork should not necessarily be discarded because the subject matter or the artists' personal history is offensive."[111] Robbins calls out a hypocrisy in American artistic studies, saying that we still read the writing of T.S Eliot who was anti-Semitic, and still watch the films of Roman Polanski who was charged with rape.

---

preservationists-trump.html.

[109] Holland Cotter, "We Need to Move, Not Destroy, Confederate Monuments," *The New York Times,* 20 Aug. 2017, https://www.nytimes.com/2017/08/20/arts/design/we-need-to-move-not-destroy-confederate-monuments.html.

[110] Dell Upton, "Confederate Monuments and Civic Values in the Wake of Charlottesville," *Society of Architectural Historians Blog,* 13 Sept. 2017, http://www.sah.org/publications-and-research/sah-blog/sah-blog/2017/09/13/confederate-monuments-and-civic-values-in-the-wake-of-charlottesville.

[111] Robin Pogrebin and Sopan Deb, "Trump Aside, Artists and Preservationists Debate the Rush to Topple Statues," *The New York Times,* 18 Aug. 2017, https://www.nytimes.com/2017/08/18/arts/design/confederate-statues-artists-preservationists-trump.html.

The prestige of these Confederate artists gives their sculptures artistic merit, and therefore, they should not be destroyed. Professionals say that these monuments also belong in historical museums. "[Museums] are full of aesthetically pleasing images of unsavory people," Dell Upton, an architectural historian, says. "They'd be quite at home there."

Upton goes further to suggest that the Confederate monuments, both those with artistic value and those without, might best be kept and displayed in a "Dead Rebels Park." When grouped together in rows upon rows, in a museum setting, like the ceramic warriors of Xi'an, the statues would create "a very powerful and thought-provoking image,".[112] According to art historians, removing the statues from their public locations in cities across the country and depositing them in museums will not remove the images' power, but re-contextualize it. The monuments' power will no longer spark oppression, but rather kindle education.

Bridget Higdon

---

[112] Dell Upton, "Confederate Monuments and Civic Values in the Wake of Charlottesville," *Society of Architectural Historians Blog*, 13 Sept. 2017, http://www.sah.org/publications-and-research/sah-blog/sah-blog/2017/09/13/confederate-monuments-and-civic-values-in-the-wake-of-charlottesville.

9 ARGUMENTS TO REMOVE THE STATUES

Acts of Vandalism

The statues are a divisive issue in groups in America. Throughout social media platforms tweets and Instagram posts and YouTube clips can be found attacking those with the opposite view. Those against the statues are indoctrinated with words of hate; they are told that they are un-American and ruining our 'culture' and the 'history' of our people.[113] Those who wish for the statues to remain are ridiculed for their backwards thinking; they are accused of being ignorant, bigoted, racist, and unwilling help America progress.[114] The lukewarm response of the government only furthers the uncertainty in the population. Instead of moving toward a peaceful compromise, those in power allow the issue to divide them as the population does as a whole. Some people have reached their boiling point with the rhetoric being spewed from both sides and have taken action to support their beliefs.

In Durham, North Carolina, protesters toppled a statue of a

---

[113] Kyle Smith, "Destroying Symbols: Where Does It End?" *National Review,* 15 Aug. 2017, www.nationalreview.com/article/450500/seo-destroying-confederate-statues-whats-end-point-washington-monument.

[114] Paul Waldman, "The Lie of Maintaining Confederate Monuments in the Name of 'History,'" *The Washington Post,* 22 Aug. 2017, www.washingtonpost.com/blogs/plum-line/wp/2017/08/22/the-lie-of-maintaining-confederate-monuments-in-the-name-of-history/?utm_term=.19d749d9bc05 ; Harriet Sinclair, "Black Lives Matter Wants a Ban on Confederate Symbols after Charlottesville Violence," *Newsweek,* 15 Aug. 2017, www.newsweek.com/black-lives-matter-ban-confederate-symbols-charlottesville-violence-651106.

Confederate soldier. The group of over one hundred chanted "No K.K.K., no fascist U.S.A." as they threw rope around the soldier's neck and tore him from his pedestal.[115] The soldier crumpled to the ground, taking a piece of his pedestal with him as he fell. The statue had stood in front of the old Durham County Courthouse with an inscription that read, "In memory of the boys who wore gray" for nearly a century. Those in the crowd protesting the statue were mostly young members of organizations such as Democratic Socialists of America, the Worker's World Party, and Industrial Workers of the World, among other anti-fascist groups. The monument was a fifteen-foot-tall reminder of the Civil War, dedicated in 1924, nearly six decades after the end of the war and in the midst of the Jim Crow era.[116] People took the situation into their own hands and removed the statue as a way of standing up for the beliefs that the government isn't fully supporting.

Another incident of vandalism occurred in Baltimore, Maryland. During the same weekend as the white nationalist rally in Charlottesville, Virginia, a one hundred fourteen year old statue was vandalized with red paint.[117] The statue was erected in February 1903 by the Daughters of the Confederacy, with the inscription "Gloria Victis", which translates to "glory to the vanquished. The paint was smeared over the Confederate soldier depicted, as well as the Confederate battle flag he holds. This isn't the first incident of vandalism for this particular statue. In 2015, it was tagged with "Black Lives Matter" after a white man killed nine black church members in South Carolina.[118] The statue, targeted because of the history it represents, has become a platform for changing political messages.

---

[115] Maggie Astor, "Protesters in Durham Topple a Confederate Monument," *The New York Times*, 14 Aug. 2017, www.nytimes.com/2017/08/14/us/protesters-in-durham-topple-a-confederate-monument.html.

[116] Ibid

[117] Tim Prudente, "Confederate Monument in Baltimore Drenched with Red Paint," *Baltimore*, 15 Aug. 2017, www.baltimoresun.com/news/maryland/baltimore-city/bs-md-ci-monument-vandalized-20170814-story.html.

[118] Ibid

Countless other monuments have been defaced, an expression of the desperation some feel to remove these objects from the public domain. In Arizona, a Jefferson Davis memorial was tarred and feathered in obvious protest of the treatment of people of color during the Confederate era.[119] A monument honoring Confederate soldiers, also in Arizona, was tagged with anti-white nationalism messages. In Florida, a West Palm Beach Confederate monument was tagged with "Nazi" and "KKK".[120] The Confederate flag carved into the monument had been chipped away. Memorial Park in Tampa was covered in red paint, splattered jarringly over the private memorial, and derogatory comments were scrawled around the monument. At Duke University, the face of a Robert E. Lee statue adorning the entrance of the university chapel was chipped off, leaving the statue irreparably damaged. After consideration, the university removed the statue permanently with the explanation that the comfort of their students was more important than the statue itself.[121] Although these acts of vandalism are varied and their receptions by the public have been divided, they send the same message: many people desire the removal of these statues. These acts of vandalism keep the issue at the forefront of people's minds; the destruction maintains the issue as relevant.

Skylar Bouffard

History of the Monuments

Many people believe that Confederate monuments, statues, and memorials represent the racist intentions of the people who built them. They promote a racist, revisionist, and untrue version of history and

---

[119] Nicole Chavez, "Monuments Vandalized after Charlottesville," *Cable News Network*, 22 Aug. 2017, www.cnn.com/2017/08/18/us/monuments-memorials-vandalized-charlottesville/index.html.

[120] Ibid

[121] Ibid

should be removed immediately.

The Southern Poverty Law Center recently published a comprehensive study of Confederate statues and monuments throughout the country. This study demonstrates that the two most popular times for building Confederate monuments were during the violent early 1900s and during the civil rights struggles of the 1950s and 60s.[122] The executive director of the American Historical Association, James Grossman, explains that "these statues were meant to create legitimate garb for white supremacy. Why would you put a statue of Robert E. Lee or Stonewall Jackson in 1948 in Baltimore?"[123]

In fact, Robert E. Lee himself opposed the creation of confederate monuments. He believed that such monuments would "anger the victorious Federals" and "would have the effect of retarding, instead of accelerating its accomplishment; and of continuing, if not adding to, the difficulties under which the Southern people labour".[124] In other words, Lee believed that the existence of confederate statues would be too divisive, which is the same reason that many people believe they should be taken down today.

The United Daughters of the Confederacy, composed of white women, was an influential organization instrumental to the construction of many Confederate memorials in the South during the late 1800s and early 1900s. This was the time of the Jim Crow laws, lynchings, race riots, and acts of violence and oppression towards African Americans. The United Daughters of the Confederacy supported this racism and

---

[122] Miles Parks, "Confederate Statues Were Built To Further A 'White Supremacist Future'," *National Public Radio*, 20 Aug. 2017, www.npr.org/2017/08/20/544266880/confederate-statues-were-built-to-further-a-white-supremacist-future.

[123] Ibid

[124] Olivia B. Waxman, "Here's Why Robert E. Lee Opposed Putting Up Confederate Monuments," *Time*, 16 Aug. 2017, time.com/4903671/charlottesville-robert-lee-confederate-monuments-history/.

built these statues to legitimize the racist regime of the time.[125]

The United Daughters of the Confederacy's goal was to honor Confederate soldiers and generals as heroes, and to promote their revisionist history of the Civil War through these statues. They referred to the Civil War as the "War Between the States", and they insisted that it was fought for the sole purpose of 'defending state's rights' rather than slavery. However, they also believed that slavery was a benevolent institution that provided African "savages" with the Christian religion, and they viewed the KKK as heroes who would return order to the South.[126] These statues were built for the purpose of representing and furthering white supremacy, not for preserving accurate history.

Furthermore, many of these statues were placed in full view of important locations for African-Americans such as former slave auction sites and courthouses, such as the Norfolk, Virginia and Virginia Beach confederate monuments.[127] These monuments were meant to send an unsettling message to anyone seeking justice from the law: that this country has and always will belong to white men, and those who do not comply with this version of America would face legal consequences.[128]

Another conspicuous location for a confederate monument is Marion Square in Charleston, West Virginia. A statue of John C. Calhoun was erected there in 1887 overlooking the newly renamed

[125] Karen L Cox, "The Whole Point of Confederate Monuments Is to Celebrate White Supremacy," *The Washington Post*, 16 Aug. 2017, www.washingtonpost.com/news/posteverything/wp/2017/08/16/the-whole-point-of-confederate-monuments-is-to-celebrate-white-supremacy/?utm_term=.2f4856c75d49.

[126] Ibid

[127] Katherine Hafner et al, "Intentional or Not, Local Confederate Monuments Were Built on or near Former Slave Sites," *The Virginian-Pilot*, 18 Aug. 2017, pilotonline.com/news/local/history/intentional-or-not-local-confederate-monuments-were-built-on-or/article_c09deef2-f83c-5181-837b-23970020b2fc.html.

[128] Miles Parks, "Confederate Statues Were Built To Further A 'White Supremacist Future'," *National Public Radio*, 20 Aug. 2017, www.npr.org/2017/08/20/544266880/confederate-statues-were-built-to-further-a-white-supremacist-future.

Calhoun Street, which happened to be home to primarily Black businesses and an important Black church (which was also the church of a slave rebellion organizer). The African-Americans in the area took that statue personally and vandalized it constantly until 1896, where it was raised to stand on top of an eight-foot column. This version of the statue still stands today.[129]

Any monument built for the purpose of furthering white supremacy does not belong in the public spaces of America. Those who defend the existence of these statues are either racist, or they are unaware of the statues' histories within the context of the United States' history.

Lily Canavan

---

[129] Dell Upton, "Confederate Monuments and Civic Values in the Wake of Charlottesville," *Society of Architectural Historians Blog*, 13 Sept. 2017, www.sah.org/publications-and-research/sah-blog/sah-blog/2017/09/13/confederate-monuments-and-civic-values-in-the-wake-of-charlottesville.

10   CONFEDERATES FEATURED IN THE STATUES

Robert E. Lee

Robert Edward Lee was born in 1807 in Stratford Hall, Virginia to a Revolutionary War veteran. Prior to the Civil War, Lee was an exceptional student at West Point; he graduated second in the class of 1829. Following his graduation, Lee served as a Captain in the Mexican-American War in 1846. Lee was then appointed as Superintendent of West Point six years later. Shortly thereafter, he was transferred as a Lieutenant Colonel to the Second Cavalry in West Texas.

At the outbreak of the Civil War in 1861, Lee resigned from his U.S. Army position in the Second Cavalry to fight for Virginia and the Confederacy. Subsequent Lee's resignation from the U.S. Army, he was appointed as Commander in Chief of the military and naval forces of Virginia. Lee was promoted once more to Brigadier General before he returned to Richmond as military advisor to President Jefferson Davis. His final position was as General for the Army of Northern Virginia. Lee fought until he was forced to surrender to Union General Ulysses S. Grant in 1865. After the war, Lee became President of Washington College, known as Washington and Lee University today. He later died at the age of 63 in Lexington, Virginia.[130]

---

[130] "Robert E. Lee," *History*, 2009, www.history.com/topics/american-civil-war/robert-e-lee ; Tanya Ballard Brown, "Who Are The Confederate Men Memorialized

Erin Varnum

J.E.B. Stuart

James Ewell Brown Stuart, or J.E.B. Stuart, was born in Patrick County, Virginia in 1833. Prior to the Civil War, Stuart graduated from West Point in 1854. He was then assigned to a unit of the U.S. Army in Texas. In 1855, shortly after his appointment in Texas, Stuart was transferred to the First Cavalry at Fort Leavenworth. At the start of the Civil War, Stuart resigned from the U.S. Army to serve as Colonel in General Stonewall Jackson's Army of the Shenandoah. Stuart was particularly skilled at providing reconnaissance, which proved to be helpful to numerous Confederate victories. Despite this overwhelming strength, he received partial blame for the Confederate defeat at Gettysburg after he failed to provide General Robert E. Lee with information regarding the Union troops' positions. Stuart was later wounded at the Battle of Yellow Tavern in 1864, prior to the end of the war. Soon after, he was taken to Richmond and subsequently died from his wounds at the age of 31.[131]

Erin Varnum

Stonewall Jackson

Thomas Jonathan Jackson, more commonly known as Stonewall Jackson, was born in 1824 in what is today part of West Virginia. After graduating from West Point, he was stationed in Mexico during the Mexican-American War. This was where he first met General Robert E. Lee. However, it wasn't until the 1861 Battle of Bull Run that Jackson became a celebrity. He earned his nickname "Stonewall" after holding his men in a strong line and prevailing despite the tremendous

---

With Statues?" *National Public Radio,* 18 Aug. 2017, www.npr.org/2017/08/18/543626600/who-are-the-confederate-men-memorialized-with-statues.

[131] "J.E.B. Stuart," *History,* 2009, www.history.com/topics/american-civil-war/j-e-b-stuart.

odds against him. This fame propelled him into leadership positions throughout the Civil War.[132] Despite his prominent role in the Confederacy, Jackson was a particularly religious man who struggled with the concept of slavery. He was especially close to the enslaved woman who had raised him. Nevertheless, Jackson accepted slavery because he believed it to be condoned by the Bible. This inspired him to start a Sunday school for slaves, both his own and those from neighboring areas.[133]

Maddie Bowe

Matthew Fontaine Maury

Virginia born Matthew Fontaine Maury gained regional fame due to his intensive study of oceanography and wind currents. He began working for the U.S. Naval Observatory and Hydrographic Office in 1842 and studied methods for decreasing ships' travel times. When the Civil War began in 1861, Maury was recruited to act as the head of coast, river, and harbor defenses for the Confederate Navy. He became most well known for his creation of the first electric mines, or "torpedoes", as Maury called them.[134] Despite the initial difficulties in implementing his plan to have offshore electric mines, these mines were the creations that destroyed the most Union naval ships. Maury's dedication to the South did not decline throughout the war. Near its end, he acted as a delegate in several European countries to advocate for the Confederacy. Even after the war ended, Maury attempted to create a colony in Mexico for Virginians and their slaves. This continued effort to sustain the pre-war way of life was both a result of misunderstanding the sentiment in post-war Virginia and of unwavering

---

[132] Charlton W. Tebeau, "Stonewall Jackson," *Encyclopædia Britannica*, 9 May 2017, www.britannica.com/biography/Stonewall-Jackson.

[133] Martha M. Boltz, "Jackson's Relation with Slaves," *The Washington Times,* 6 Apr. 2007, www.washingtontimes.com/news/2007/apr/6/20070406-103241-8494r/.

[134] "Matthew Fontaine Maury," *Encyclopædia Britannica*, 27 Feb. 2017, www.britannica.com/biography/Matthew-Fontaine-Maury.

commitment to the Southern cause and the sustainment of slavery as an institution.[135]

Maddie Bowe

Jefferson Davis

Jefferson Davis was born in 1808 in Kentucky. He was raised in Mississippi, where he later owned a plantation. Davis was a vocal supporter of the institution of slavery and its economic importance in the South. After graduating from West Point, Davis was elected to the House of Representatives. He left in order to serve in the Mexican-American War. After the war ended in 1853, Davis was appointed as the U.S. Secretary of War. Only four years later, he became a Mississippi senator and a vocal proponent of states' rights. He left office at the onset of the Civil War, when he was picked as the President of the Confederacy. Despite not desiring the position himself, the selection of Davis represented a choice that pacified both moderate and radical factions of the Confederacy. However, his popularity was brief, as his short temper and tendency to promote loyalty over success did not aid in rectifying the damage done by an increasing number of Confederate defeats. Davis was forced to flee Richmond in April of 1865 and was captured in Georgia during May of the same year . He was never able to return to the Senate because he refused to request a pardon for his actions during the Civil War.[136]

Maddie Bowe

Marion Sims

While not directly involved in the Civil War, Marion Sims, born in 1813, is frequently referenced in the debate surrounding the

---

[135] "Electrical Excursions of Mathew Fontaine Maury (1806-1873)," *Engineering and Technology History Wiki*, 15 Sept. 2016, ethw.org/Electrical_Excursions_of_Mathew_Fontaine_Maury_(1806-1873).

[136] "Jefferson Davis," *Civil War Trust*, www.civilwar.org/learn/biographies/jefferson-davis.

Confederate monuments. As "the father of modern gynecology", Sims made a number of important discoveries related to female surgical practices. He was renowned as a surgeon throughout the U.S. and Europe, particularly for inventing the speculum and pioneering surgery for fistula. However, his achievements are tainted by the fact that some of his innovations arose from performing experiments on enslaved black women without anesthesia.[137]

Nicky Paulson

---

[137] "J. Marion Sims," *Wikipedia*, 6 Nov. 2017, en.wikipedia.org/wiki/J._Marion_Sims.

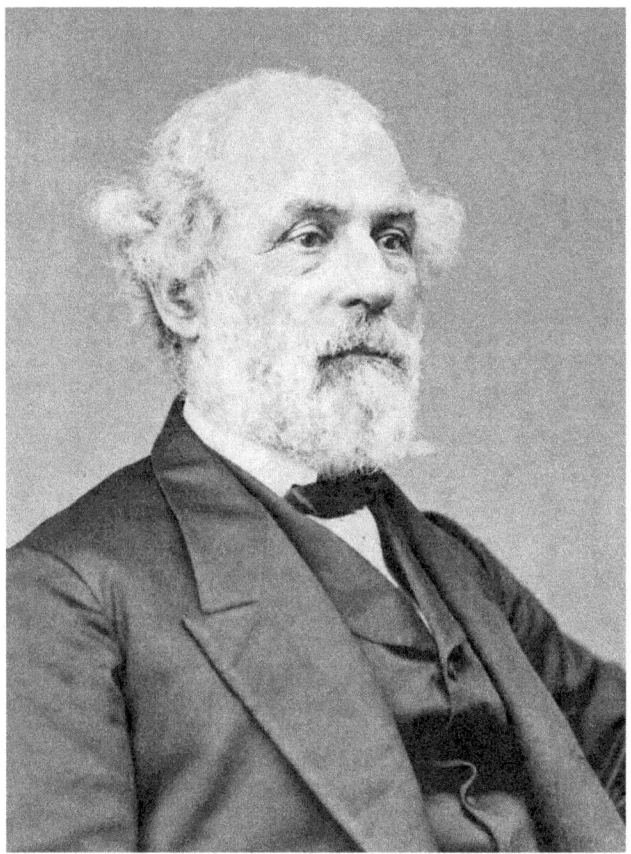

Robert E. Lee[138]

---

[138] Matthew Brady. *Robert E. Lee in his postbellum years.* 1867. Photograph. Available from: Wikimedia Commons, https://commons.wikimedia.org/wiki/File:Robert_Lee_-_postbellum.jpg

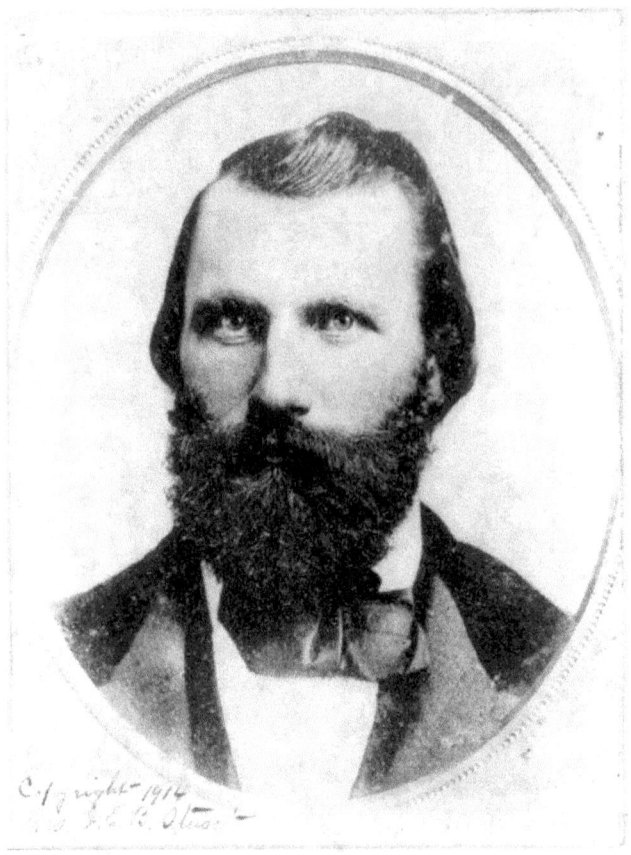

J.E.B. Stuart[139]

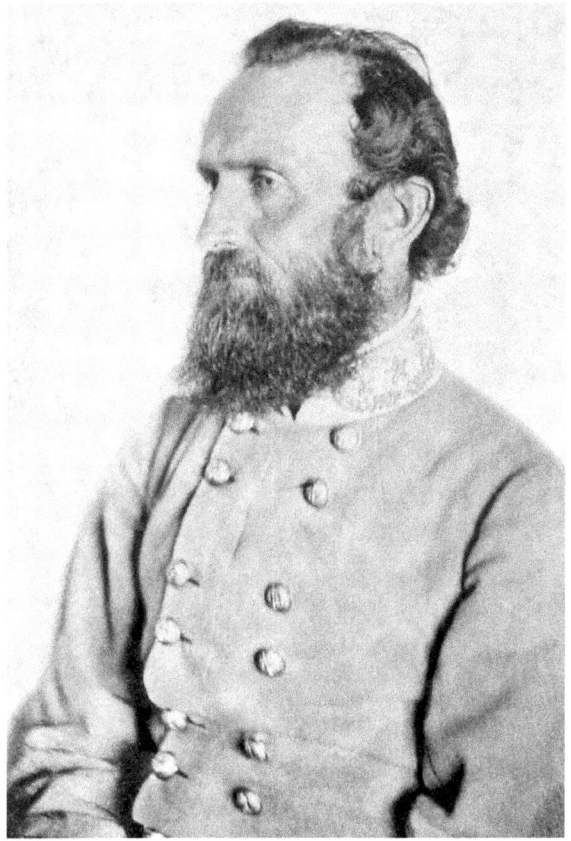

Stonewall Jackson[140]

[140] *General Jackson's "Chancellorsville" Portrait.* 26 April 1863. Photograph. Available from: Wikimedia Commons, https://commons.wikimedia.org/wiki/File:Stonewall_Jackson.jpg

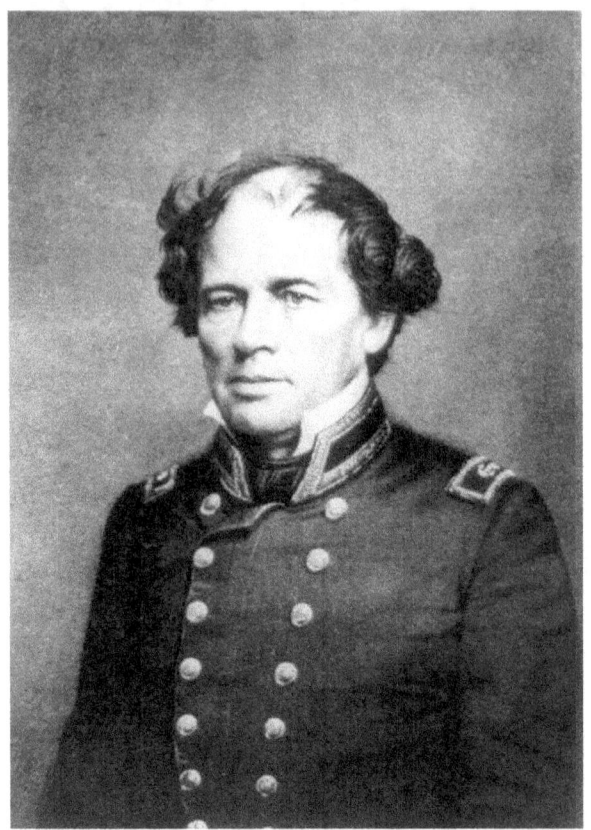

Matthew Fontaine Maury[141]

[141] *Matthew Fontaine Maury as a U.S. Navy Lieutenant.* 1853. Photograph. Available from: Wikimedia Commons,
https://commons.wikimedia.org/wiki/File:Lt._Matthew_Maury.jpg

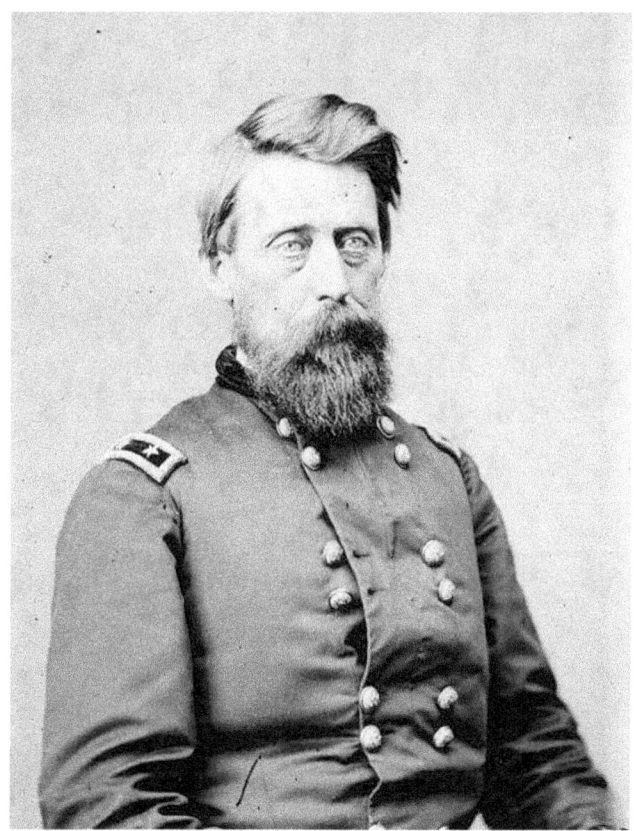

Jefferson Davis[142]

[142] *Major General Jefferson C. Davis.* 1860-1870. Photograph. Available from: Wikimedia Commons, https://commons.wikimedia.org/wiki/File:Jefferson_C._Davis.jpg

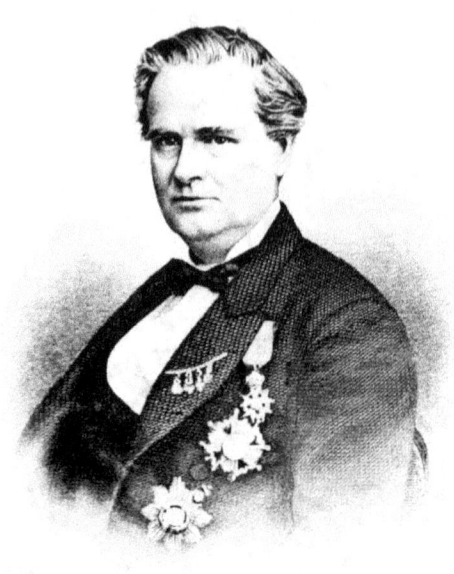

Marion Sims[143]

———————————

[143] *Portrait of James M. Sims wearing orders and decorations.* Portrait. Available from: Wikimedia Commons,
https://commons.wikimedia.org/wiki/File:Portrait_of_James_M._Sims_wearing_orders_an
d_decorations._Wellcome_M0010059.jpg

CONCLUSION

In the United States, it is a human right to be able to express opinions freely, without restraint and without reprimand. As permitted by the First Amendment to the United States Constitution, opinions can be conveyed in whatever way deemed most suitable - whether that be through speech, protest, or art - without fear of censorship.

The Confederate statues that were erected across the American landscape in the early part of the twentieth century were vehicles through which certain individuals shared their beliefs and values with the greater nation. Since the construction of these monuments, their presence has brought both great pride and great pain to different groups of people.

In recent months, Americans have raised handmade signs high over their heads, protesting for the preservation or removal of the Confederate statues. In August 2017, the protests in Charlottesville escalated beyond civil protests to physical violence, leaving one woman dead.

As result, a month later, the city of Charlottesville voted to tear down its statue of Stonewall Jackson. The statue of Robert E. Lee will also be removed. Other cities have since followed suit. The mayor of Baltimore decided to remove all Confederate monuments from the city's public spaces, and in November 2017 in New Orleans, an enormous statue of an African American woman was erected on the pedestal where a monument to Jefferson Davis previously stood.[144]

While many Confederate monuments have yet to be taken down, Americans are beginning to realize that when opinions, speech, protest,

---

[144] Doug MacCash, "Statue of Woman Appears Where Jefferson Davis Monument Once Stood," *NOLA*, 13 Nov. 2017, www.nola.com/arts/index.ssf/2017/11/jefferson_davis_monument_video.html.

or art hurts others – stabs the heart till it bleeds its American colors – those opinions are no longer allowed to be free.

The Confederate generals and soldiers who are memorialized in these controversial statues are frozen in time. They are enshrined mid-stride, mid-salute, or mid-speech. But nonetheless, these men speak to us. And we must decide, as a nation, whether their message is one we wish to continue to hear.

Bridget Higdon

TIMELINE OF EVENTS

January 1861: After Lincoln is elected President, South Carolina secedes from the states, quickly followed by Florida, Mississippi, Georgia, Alabama, Louisiana and Texas. Those states are later joined by Virginia, Arkansas, Tennessee and North Carolina, forming the Confederate States of America.[145]

April 12ᵗʰ 1861: The Battle of Fort Sumter occurs, the first battle of the Civil War.[146]

September 22ⁿᵈ 1862: Lincoln issued a preliminary Emancipation Proclamation, warning that as of January 1, 1863 all slaves in rebellious states would be considered free.[147]

April 9ᵗʰ 1865: General Robert E. Lee surrenders to Ulysses S. Grant, ending the Civil War.[148]

December 6ᵗʰ 1865: The 13ᵗʰ Amendment was established, officially abolishing slavery.[149]

1865-1866: The former Confederate States put in place 'black codes,' a series of laws meant to limit the freedom of newly freed slaves.[150]

1866: Formation of the Ku Klux Klan.[151]

---

[145] "Civil War Timeline," *HistoryNet*, www.historynet.com/civil-war-timeline.

[146] Ibid

[147] Ibid

[148] Ibid

[149] Ibid

[150] "Civil Rights Timeline between 1951-1969," *Laws*, kids.laws.com/civil-rights-timeline.

[151] Ibid

July 9ᵗʰ 1868: The 14ᵗʰ Amendment is ratified, expanding on the 13ᵗʰ Amendment and guaranteeing equal treatment under the law to all citizens.[152]

1890: Centerpiece of Monument Avenue unveiled, equestrian statue of Robert E. Lee.

1894: Daughters of the Confederacy formed.

1896: Plessy v. Ferguson.[153]

May 1907: A statue General James Ewell Brown Stuart was unveiled on Monument Avenue.

June 1907: A statue of Jefferson Davis was unveiled on Monument Avenue.

1912: Two plaques commemorating Robert E. Lee and funded by the Daughter's of the Confederacy are placed next to a tree Lee had been painted near in Brooklyn.

1915: Revival of the Ku Klux Klan.[154]

1919: A statue of General Thomas Jonathan Jackson was unveiled on Monument Avenue.

Summer 1919: Red Summer. A series of race riots across the country resulted in over 165 deaths.[155]

May 31ˢᵗ-June 1ˢᵗ 1921: Greenwood Race Riot. Black Wall Street destroyed out of envy and bitterness.[156]

---

[152] Ibid

[153] Ibid

[154] Ibid

[155] Ibid

[156] Ibid

October 19ᵗʰ 1921: An equestrian statue of Thomas "Stonewall" Jackson was unveiled in what was at the time Jackson Park, Charlottesville, VA. The Park is now known as Justice Park.

1923: The Daughter's of the Confederacy convince the Bronx Community College to place a bust of Robert E. Lee in their Hall of Fame for Great Americans.

May 21ˢᵗ 1924: A statue of Robert E. Lee was unveiled in Emancipation Park, known as Lee Park at the time, Charlottesville, VA.

1929: A Confederate scientist Matthew Fontaine Maury was honored with a statue on Monument Avenue.

1931: Stone monument is erected to confederate soldiers in a confederate graveyard in Madison, WI.

1954: Brown v. Board of Education.[157]

1957: The Daughter's of the Confederacy convince the Bronx Community College to place a bust of Stonewall Jackson in their Hall of Fame for Great Americans.

1964: Civil Rights Act.[158]

1997: Monument Avenue was declared a National Historic Landmark.

1981: A privately funded and installed plaque is placed in a confederate graveyard in Madison, WI. It uses problematic language, calling the soldiers "unsung heroes" and "valiant."

May 11ᵗʰ 2017: A statue of Jefferson Davis is removed from public New Orleans in the middle of the night. It is currently in a warehouse awaiting a decision.

---

[157] Ibid

[158] Ibid

August 2017: The Madison, WI graveyard plaque is removed.

August 16ᵗʰ 2017: Two plaques in Brooklyn commemorating Robert E. Lee are removed.

August 18ᵗʰ 2017: The Bronx Community College removes the busts of both Jackson and Lee from their collection.

September 2017: Charlottesville makes the decision to tear down the statues of both Robert E. Lee and "Stonewall" Jackson, although no action has yet been taken.

Skylar Bouffard

STUDENTS OF ART AND ITS DESTRUCTION

Kate Bamberger—English
Sarah Boller—Biology
Skylar Bouffard—Neuroscience
Maddie Bowe—Economics
Lily Canavan—Environmental Science
Michael Chan—Business Administration
Emily Connolly—English
Meagan Cummins—Chemistry
Bridget Higdon—English
Zoë Kalbag—Microbiology
Kyle McLaughlin—Biological Science
Ally Merril—Neuroscience
Cali Murray—Biological Science
Joscie Norris—Environmental Science
Nicky Paulson—Psychological Science
Sean Quigley—Molecular Genetics
Emma Roach—German
Erin Varnum—Anthropology

www.ingramcontent.com/pod-product-compliance
Lightning Source LLC
Chambersburg PA
CBHW071216220526
45468CB00002B/631